Beautiful Inheritance

A 101-Day Devotional

MARILYN HICKEY

Beautiful Inheritance
101 Days to Knowing Who You Are and What You Possess As a Child of God

Copyright © 2022 Marilyn Hickey Ministries.

Marilyn Hickey Ministries
PO Box 6598
Englewood, CO 80155–6598

marilynandsarah.org

Compiled and edited by: Bobbie Sartini and Sarah Heaton

Illustrated by: Manal Fashi

ISBN: 978-1-938696-28-2

Assembled and Produced for Marilyn Hickey Ministries by
Breakfast for Seven
2150 E. Continental Blvd., Southlake, TX 76092
breakfastforseven.com

CONTENTS

NOTE TO THE READER

As you read through these daily devotions, we've included illustrations that were created to inspire you in your daily walk with the Lord. These watercolor images revolve around garden scenes and symbols such as planting seeds, watering, harvesting, and taking in the beauty that is our inheritance from God.

It is our hope and prayer that just like the garden scenes shown, your time reading these devotions will bring growth and fruit into your life.

A WORD FROM MARILYN

We know we can't always live on the mountaintops. Even as we walk through the valleys of our lives and encounter days that drag us down, God has given us multiple weapons to help us climb back up to the mountain heights. For starters, we have God's wisdom, Word, and anointing.

But that's not all God has provided for us. There is one ultimate weapon that works on everything! In Romans 8:35–39, the apostle Paul says that this ultimate weapon will work on 17 different threats to our well-being. It will work on tribulation, distress, persecution, famine, and nakedness. It is guaranteed to make us victorious over peril, sword, death or life, angels, principalities, and powers. And it even works wonders on things present and things to come, on heights and depths, and on "any other created thing."

What then is this ultimate weapon? It is your knowledge of God's love for you—knowing how well and how much God loves you. Once you are fully persuaded of God's love for you, there is nothing, and I mean nothing, that could happen to you or your loved ones that would keep you from walking in victory every day of your life—and on into eternity, to enjoy a life completely enveloped by the love of God.

My goal for you in going through these daily devotions is that you will begin to take hold of God's love for you, your loved ones, and the world. The Christian life is a life of love and compassion. By applying God's love and compassion to your life's circumstances along with some of the spiritual and practical insights I have learned throughout my decades of walking with the Lord, you can be empowered to do the supernatural. You, too, can become a world changer!

Throughout the pages of this devotional, you can discover the purpose and meaning of your life. In addition, as you pray through your trials and tribulations, I believe you can find God's strength in your weaknesses. As you step into God's plans and role for your life, I pray that your knowledge of God's love for you will increase, your faith will work to transform your circumstances and move mountains, and that more grace will abound to you and through you. After all, these are all just a small part of your *beautiful inheritance* as a Christian.

Covenant

Open-Heart Surgery

In Him you were also circumcised with the circumcision
made without hands, by putting off the body of the
sins of the flesh, by the circumcision of Christ.

(COLOSSIANS 2:11)

*D*o you realize that when you were born-again, you had "open-heart" surgery? This is a spiritual "operation" that the Bible likens to the Jewish rite of circumcision. It's a "circumcised heart." When you are born-again, you receive your new nature, your heart is "circumcised," and you are marked for God.

In the Jewish faith, circumcision is the ceremony that marks the baby as belonging to God and a partaker in the covenant between God and Abraham (see Genesis 17:10–11). When Abraham circumcised his household, he established his seed forever as set apart for God. Circumcision of the heart is so important that God Himself performs the "operation." When God circumcises your heart, a covenant is established between you and God. Colossians 2:11–12 tells us:

*In Him you were also circumcised with the
circumcision made without hands, by putting
off the body of the sins of the flesh, by the
circumcision of Christ, ... through faith in the
working of God, who raised Him from the dead.*

Think about it. Ishmael was born before Abraham was circumcised; Isaac wasn't born until after he was circumcised. Ishmael was born out of the flesh nature, but Isaac was born out of his spirit nature. The "Isaacs" of your life will only be born after your heart is circumcised.

Open-heart surgery (circumcision of the heart) refers to cutting off the lust and passion of the flesh so you can hear from God and His new nature can come into you. Your old, flesh nature can only produce Ishmaels. But your new nature in Christ produces new beginnings! When you are born-again, God opens your heart to the things of the Lord, and nothing is impossible through Jesus. You are also given a new name—"Christian"—and your name is written in the Lamb's Book of Life! The circumcised heart marks you for victory. When your heart is circumcised, *"He who is in you is greater than he who is in the world"* (1 John 4:4).

God wants you to serve Him. However, no man can serve God in the flesh. You might say, "I love God. I was born into a Christian home. I have a heart for God. I'm going to serve Him." But if you're not born-again, then you're only going to produce works for God out of your flesh, which profits nothing (see John 6:63). A circumcised heart gives you a new nature with which to serve God.

The circumcised heart is open to the things of God, brings about your new nature, protects you, and marks you for victory rather than defeat. Are you walking in defeat? Are you living in the flesh? Do you desire to change your life, hear from God, and start walking in victory, protection, and a new way of life? Then tell God you want to have "open-heart" surgery. You can do it right now by praying this prayer with me:

> Father, I come to you desiring a new life with you. I confess my sins, and I believe that I am forgiven through the blood of Jesus. I claim Jesus as the minister of your promises to me. I choose to cut off the passions and lusts of the flesh and claim my new nature whereby I can hear from you. In Jesus's name, amen.

Our Jealous God

"For you shall worship no other god, for the LORD,
whose name is Jealous, is a jealous God."
(EXODUS 34:14)

When you really love someone, you do a lot of special little things that you know will please the other person. That's the way God is with us—and He wants to be your first love. He wants to be the center of your life; He wants you to love Him more than anything or anybody else. He wants you to commit your love to Him because He has committed His love to you.

When you are born-again, you enter into a covenant relationship with God, becoming one with Him; you belong to Him, and He belongs to you. God has agreed to protect you and watch over you as a husband would for his wife. Just as in marriage, if you begin to wander away from your first love, God will become jealous. In fact, His name is "Jealous": *"For you shall worship no other god, for the LORD, whose name is Jealous, is a jealous God"* (Exodus 34:14). God is concerned about your relationship with Him. He knows that when you begin to put other things before Him, little by little, you will be drawn further away from Him; and that makes Him jealous.

When we don't appreciate God's love, He reacts like a jealous husband. Nahum 1:2 says, *"God is jealous, and the LORD avenges; . . . and is furious. The LORD will take vengeance on His adversaries, and He reserves wrath for His enemies."* Those who oppose God will experience His wrath. Those who come against God's covenant people oppose Him and will also experience God's wrath. Your heavenly Father loves you and will fight against your enemies.

When you enter into a covenant relationship with Him, God will look out for your welfare. At the same time, God will become angry if you "two-time" Him. He wants to be your first love. He is a jealous lover, and He wants your total commitment to Him. If you really love someone, you want to be around that person all the time, right? If you are slack in how you treat God—if you read your Bible only when it's convenient for you, or if you prefer to sleep in rather than to get up for church on Sunday—how do you think God feels? As the Scripture says, He will become jealous. But even in jealousy, His compassions never fail.

Ezekiel 39:25 illustrates this beautifully, *"Therefore thus says the Lord GOD: 'Now I will bring back the captives of Jacob, and have mercy on the whole house of Israel; and I will be jealous for My holy name.'"* Here, God is referring to Israel's 70 years of captivity in Babylon. Because Israel is God's covenant people,

His jealousy provoked Him to mercy. God said, "Yes, they blew it; but I love them. Out of my mercy, I will bring them back!" And God will do the same for you, too.

God's covenant with Israel assures His protection over Israel even to this day. Nowadays, many Jews are very traditional but not very religious. God wants to protect Israel because they are His covenant people. He looks out for their welfare and safety even though they don't really know Him. God's love for His people is so overwhelming that His jealousy provokes His mercy. The same is true for you. He will show you mercy when you are in a covenant relationship with Him.

Zealousness

The zeal of the LORD of hosts will perform this.
(ISAIAH 9:7)

A zealous person is always busy, always seeking to get something accomplished. A zealous Christian seeks after God and the things of God. That's because zeal performs. Isaiah writes:

> *Of the increase of His government and peace there will be no end, upon the throne of David and over His kingdom, to order it and establish it with judgment and justice from that time forward, even forever. The zeal of the LORD of hosts will perform this.* **(ISAIAH 9:7)**

The word for zeal in Hebrew is *qin'â* which means "jealousy, envy, or zeal." Jealousy and zeal are very similar. Your zealousness for the Lord begins when you want God more than anything else in the world. When you love someone, you desire to be like that person. Likewise, there is a zeal for God and a jealousy for the things of God that makes us say, "God, I want to love what you love, and go after what you want to go after."

What does God want to go after? Titus 2:14 tells us that Jesus *"gave Himself for us, that He might redeem us from every lawless deed and purify for Himself His own special people, zealous for good works."* These good works are the very things that God is zealous over, and His number-one priority is sinners. His zeal is such that He gave Jesus to die for us and to redeem us from our sins.

When Jesus went into the temple and cast out the money changers, His disciples saw the words of Psalm 69:9 in His actions, *"Because zeal for Your house has eaten me up."* (See also John 2:17.) Jesus was so consumed with love for His Father's house that in the natural, it looked like He must have gone mad. Yet, in reality, Jesus was upset because the money changers were taking advantage of the people. They weren't praying for the sick, healing the brokenhearted, or counseling and ministering to people in need. These "merchants" didn't care if people got anything from the heart of God. They just wanted money. Jesus threw them out because their zeal was not for the things of God.

A wonderful, modern-day example of zealousness for God happened in India. Some years ago, a man named Chawnga followed the missionary who had led him to Christ to another province where he learned to read and write. Because of his zeal for God, he ended up evangelizing his tribe—80 percent of the tribe converted to Christianity. Not satisfied, he sent his son, Rochunga ("Ro"), away to school so that he could translate the New Testament into their language. When he finished college, his zeal for God led him to study in Britain, then Wheaton College in Illinois. Ro translated the New Testament and took it back to his people; despite threats against his life, he got 10,000 copies into India. Ro had great zeal to do more for God. One night, he dreamed of God telling him to send New Testaments to everyone in the phone books. With help from the American Bible Society, 50,000 Bibles were sent. Some 20,000 Hindus, Muslims, and others responded. Ro's zeal consumed him. This was the beginning of the organization called Bibles for the World. This one man's zeal led to a lifetime of commitment to reach the world with God's Word.

God wants you to give your heart totally to Him, to be filled with a zeal for Him, to pursue Him and be abundantly fruitful for Him, now and forever. Pray and tell God that you totally surrender to Him anything in you that is holding you back from Him and make Him the object of your zeal.

Covenant Relationship

*If you are Christ's, then you are Abraham's
seed, and heirs according to the promise.*

(GALATIANS 3:29)

God wants to bless you through Abraham's covenant! Now, you may be thinking, "How could I be included in a covenant given to Abraham and his descendants? I don't have a drop of Jewish blood in my veins." Neither do I. Yet, the Bible says that God considers us sons and daughters of Abraham and rightful heirs to Abraham's covenant benefits.

Look at Galatians 3:7: *"... those who are of faith are sons of Abraham."* Now look at Galatians 3:29: *"If you are Christ's, then you are Abraham's seed, and heirs according to the promise."* Do you belong to Christ? If you are born-again, then you are a son or daughter of Abraham! As his "heir," you have every right to the four blessings of the Abrahamic Covenant.

God wants more than a ritualistic or ceremonial relationship with mankind. He desires a warm, intimate, person-to-person, family connection with you. God called Abraham His "friend," and He wants to call you His friend, too. Jesus expressed it this way, *"No longer do I call you servants, for a servant does not know what his master is doing; but I have called you friends"* (John 15:15).

Every person on the face of the earth—no matter their religion or even if they are atheists—is only one short prayer away from entering into Abraham's covenant. Salvation—accepting that you are a sinner and receiving the blood of Christ as the source of forgiveness from sin—is the only way to be included in Abraham's "bloodline." If you haven't done that, or if you have drifted away from your relationship with God, you can establish or reestablish it in a single moment with one short prayer from your heart. If you would like to do that right now, pray with me:

Dear heavenly Father, forgive me of my sins.
Wash me clean through the blood of Jesus.
Forgive me for ever doubting that you want to
give me the best possible life. I receive Jesus as
Lord of my life—the provider of my salvation,
my prosperity, my healing, and blessings for
my family. I want an intimate relationship with
you, Jesus. Come into my heart and make me
a new person. In Jesus's name, I pray. Amen.

You are now in a covenant relationship with God through
the blood of Jesus that was shed on the cross. Ancient covenants were confirmed by blood. At God's request, Abraham
sacrificed animals to memorialize God's covenant with
him (see Genesis 15:6–21). We, however, were adopted into
Abraham's covenant through the blood of Christ shed for our
sins. Our covenant is a legal, binding relationship between
two parties—us and God.

You, like Abraham, are a child and friend of God, and a joint
heir with Christ: *"We are children of God, and if children, then
heirs—heirs of God and joint heirs with Christ"* (Romans 8:16–17).
Out of our covenant relationship with God springs obedience.
Out of God's covenant relationship with us flows blessings,
which we'll look at tomorrow.

Covenant Blessings

"I will make you a great nation; I will bless you and make your name great; and you shall be a blessing. I will bless those who bless you, and I will curse him who curses you; and in you all the families of the earth shall be blessed."

(GENESIS 12:2–3)

Because of his covenant with God, Abraham received many blessings and promises, which unfolded over a span of time. Genesis 12:2–3 tells us the first part. When God told Abraham to leave his country and his father's house and go to a land He would show him, He promised: *"I will make you a great nation; I will bless you and make your name great; and you shall be a blessing. I will bless those who bless you, and I will curse him who curses you; and in you all the families of the earth shall be blessed"* (Genesis 12:2–3). This covenant was expanded after Abraham returned from Egypt following a famine—he and his descendants were given a land grant—Israel. Then in Genesis 22:17–18, following Abraham's willingness to sacrifice his son Isaac, God enlarged the covenant. His descendants would be so many that they couldn't be counted, and Genesis 22:17 says they would *"possess the gate of their enemies."*

If you categorize all the blessings, you will find that they affect four areas of life. God wants to bless the same four areas of your life.

- Spiritual Blessing: God wants to bless you with eternal life and friendship. He wants a personal relationship with you.
- Financial Blessing: God wants to bless you with material possessions, just as he did Abraham, Isaac, and Jacob.
- Physical Blessing: God wants to bless you with health and long life. You are not at the mercy of illness and premature death.
- Family Blessing: God wants to bless your children and grandchildren. If you tell the devil to back off and leave your family alone, he has to obey.

Unfortunately, there are covenant casualties. One of the saddest characters in the Bible is Isaac's son, Esau, *who for one morsel of food sold his birthright"* (Hebrews 12:16). He had so

little respect for the covenant that he received only a tiny portion of the blessing which was his birthright. Unfortunately, some Christians do the same as Esau. In ignorance or disbelief, they miss out on their full covenant benefits. Believing that God's plan was only to meet their *greatest* need (forgiveness of sin) rather than *all* their needs, they receive only the spiritual benefit of salvation.

Covenant benefits are not automatic. Like salvation, they must be received by faith. Consequently, those who do not understand their covenant may needlessly suffer sickness and poverty or watch helplessly as loved ones' lives are ruined by Satan. Don't let that happen to you! As a partaker of Abraham's covenant, Romans 5:17 says that you can *"reign in life through the One, Jesus Christ."* Let me encourage you—be a covenant partaker!

Know Your Covenant Rights

"Your servant has killed both lion and bear; and this uncircumcised Philistine will be like one of them, seeing he has defied the armies of the living God."

(1 SAMUEL 17:36)

*H*ave you ever felt that life is one giant problem after another? It doesn't have to be! You can use God's power on the biggest difficulty and see it dissolve, never to return. God wants to make impossibilities bow down to you, and He wants to put giant problems under your feet. Regardless of their size, you can overcome the worst circumstances if you will follow David's example.

Despite Goliath's size, David, a young shepherd, was able to kill him because David knew his covenant rights. In fact, he may have been the only one in Israel at that time who was willing to act on God's covenant promises. The Israelites seemed to be focused on the problem instead of the solution; they felt defeated already. But when David heard the giant Goliath raging in the valley, his response was: *"Who is this uncircumcised Philistine, that he should defy the armies of the living God?"*

(1 Samuel 17:26). David immediately claimed his covenant rights obtained through circumcision. He was saying, "This man doesn't have a covenant with God, but we do!"

As soon as David expressed his reliance on God's promises, even his own brother rebuked him. There may be times when your family or friends will oppose you. King Saul didn't think that David could fight, let alone slay the giant. David told him, *"Your servant has killed both lion and bear; and this uncircumcised Philistine will be like one of them, seeing he has defied the armies of the living God"* (1 Samuel 17:36).

When your family or others come against you, don't allow their unbelief to prevent you from living a life of faith. Establish yourself in God's Word and in His promises. Rehearse your past victories to encourage your spirit and strengthen you to fight the present battle—and come out on top. Whenever the devil launches an attack, remember that he's not after you; he's after God! David knew that, so he could confidently proclaim, "God's going to win!"

You, too, are in a covenant relationship with God. Romans 2:29 says that our *"circumcision is that of the heart, in the spirit."* As a child of God, you have been promised many wonderful things; Jesus has promised you His peace, wisdom, abundance, and so much more! When giant problems come along to steal those promises, be like David—stand firm in your covenant position.

The Benefits of Adoption

*You did not receive the spirit of bondage again
to fear, but you received the Spirit of adoption
by whom we cry out, "Abba, Father."*

(ROMANS 8:15)

Many Christians know they've been born-again, but they don't realize they've been adopted as well. As a Christian, you have been made a son of God by adoption (Galatians 4:5). Adoption means that you were delivered from the slavery and bondage of sin. Romans 8:15 says, *"You did not receive the spirit of bondage again to fear, but you received the Spirit of adoption by whom we cry out, 'Abba, Father.'"* Abba means "daddy." You were born as a slave to sin. Before Jesus came, we were in bondage, but now we have been redeemed. Your adoption made you a child of God.

God even planned your adoption! Ephesians 1:5 says that **God chose you**: *"Having predestined us to adoption as sons by Jesus Christ to Himself, according to the good pleasure of His will."* Before God made the world, He planned for your adoption. Your salvation was not predestined—it was your choice—but your adoption was predestined and was very expensive. You were so polluted, dark, and sinful that somebody had to die in your place to get you out of the mess. That somebody was the one whom God loved the most, His dear Son Jesus: *"God sent forth His Son, . . . to redeem those who were under the law, that we might receive the adoption as sons"* (Galatians 4:4–5). The price for you was Jesus's blood. Jesus is the Son of God, but He became the Son of Man. You were born a son of man, but Jesus's sacrifice made you a son of God.

God adopts everyone who is saved and grants them the privileges of His family relationship. As a son, you possess all the family rights, privileges, conditions, and authority. Spiritual adoption is far superior to natural adoption because you are entitled to all the things your Father has:

- You get His character traits. When God adopts you, you gradually begin to look and act like Him because the Spirit who knows the Father and calls Him "Daddy" enters your heart. So, you begin to look, act, and speak like Him.
- Your adoption has made you an heir. When you were born-again, you exchanged slavery for sonship, and you received all that Jesus has as an heir (see Romans 8:17).

- First John 3:1 says, *"Behold what manner of love the Father has bestowed on us, that we should be called children of God! Therefore the world does not know us, because it did not know Him."* The world won't understand that God is more familiar to you than any natural father could ever be. But God made you an heir because He is a Daddy who believes in taking care of His children.
- Many Christians are in bondage to insecurity, but you do not have to be insecure. Let God take the graveclothes of fear from you and give you His security blanket of adoption.
- Through adoption you can be secure about your past and present, and you can also be secure for all eternity. Jesus said, *"You did not choose Me, but I chose you . . ."* (John 15:16). The best part is that when you chose Him, He wrote your name in His Book of Life.

God loves you as much as He loves Jesus. God didn't choose you because you were worthy; He chose you because He's wild over you and He wants you to overcome! Every time you get a miracle in your life, you can know that Daddy gave you that miracle because you believed what the Spirit inside you was saying: "Daddy! Daddy!"

The Master's Hands

Resurrection Power

But if the Spirit of Him who raised Jesus from the dead dwells in you, He who raised Christ from the dead will also give life to your mortal bodies through His Spirit who dwells in you.

(ROMANS 8:11)

*I*f you are a member of the family of Christ, you are heir to an immense inheritance that Jesus put in trust for you almost 2,000 years ago when He rose from the grave and conquered death. When you were born-again, this inheritance—far more valuable than silver or gold—became yours. With His resurrection, Jesus broke a threefold curse of death. Consequently, when you accepted Him as your Lord and Savior, you inherited a threefold right to life.

When Adam sinned, he died spiritually. Sin separated him from God and brought spiritual death to the whole human race. Jesus broke that curse, so you inherited a right to spiritual life, *"For as in Adam all die, even so in Christ all shall be made alive"* (1 Corinthians 15:22). Additionally, Adam's sin brought the consequence of physical death. Jesus also broke that curse by literally overcoming His physical mortality. Part of your resurrection legacy is the right to physical life in your body—and eternal life through His Spirit: *"But if the Spirit of Him who raised Jesus from the dead dwells in you, He who raised Christ from the dead will also give life to your mortal bodies through His Spirit who dwells in you"* (Romans 8:11).

Finally, you have inherited a full provision for healing through Christ's sacrifice that guarantees you the right to a healthy life. Jesus *"bore our sins in His own body on the tree, that we, having died to sins, might live for righteousness—by whose stripes you were healed"* (1 Peter 2:24). God repeatedly stresses in His Word that Jesus died for your health. Matthew 8:17 says, *"He Himself took our infirmities and bore our sicknesses."* Healing is a major part of atonement. Deuteronomy 28:15–68 shows that the curse included all manner of diseases and distresses, but by His death and resurrection, Jesus redeemed us from the curse of the law (see Galatians 3:13).

By overcoming death, Jesus left you the legacy of resurrection power. This is one of the most exciting gifts He has for you. You received it when you were born-again for the purpose of transforming your soul. No wonder Philippians 2:13 can say, *"For it is God who works in you both to will and to do for His good pleasure."* God has put resurrection power to work in your spirit, soul, and body.. The covenant made by the death and resurrection of Jesus provides for your spiritual and physical needs, including your transformation, purification, eternal life, spiritual energy, and power. It provides emergency provisions, divine protection, reconciliation—and the very presence of God!

Resurrection power gives you the means of rising from the death of your old ways to a new and glorious life in Jesus Christ. Have you ever heard people who think they will never be able to change? You may have even felt that way yourself. Christ's resurrection power gives you a wonderful advantage, for it guarantees your spiritual transformation. You pass from death in sin to life in Christ—and all things become possible!

From the moment you accept Jesus as your Lord and Savior, this resurrection power is yours—this incredible inheritance is really yours! The Word is your Father's will, and all His promises and legacies are there for you to read. I encourage you to do so. As a child of God, you became rich beyond measure when Jesus rose from the grave. You can now walk in victory every day of your life because you have the authority, Word, blood, and resurrection power of Christ to guarantee your threefold right to life!

Profiting from Jesus's Ascension

"Nevertheless I tell you the truth. It is to your advantage that I go away; for if I do not go away, the Helper will not come to you; but if I depart, I will send Him to you."

(JOHN 16:7)

*I*t is so important for you to understand the benefits not only of Jesus's resurrection, but also of His ascension. His resurrection points to life after death, and whatever He touches, He will enrich and bring to life. His ascension, however, is also key to our Christian walk. At His ascension, Jesus was taken up in the clouds because He was going to touch the earth in a special way. Before He left, Jesus told His followers that He would send the Holy Spirit. Then, on Pentecost, 120 of His followers were baptized in the Holy Spirit. Jesus went up, and the Holy Spirit came down and touched the earth—and He's still working in the earth today.

Through the work of the Holy Spirit, the Church is producing fruit in God's kingdom. The gifts He gives us could not be given until after Christ had returned to His Father.

In John 16:7, Jesus said it was to our "advantage" that He go away: *"Nevertheless I tell you the truth. It is to your advantage that I go away; for if I do not go away, the Helper will not come to you; but if I depart, I will send Him to you"* (John 16:7).

The Greek word translated as "advantage" is *sympherō* and means "profitable." We profited through Jesus's ascension because now the Holy Spirit works through us. Furthermore, when Jesus ascended, He was no longer localized. Through the power of the Holy Spirit, Jesus is no longer restricted to geographic boundaries. He is everywhere, living in the hearts of men and working to produce fruit.

The fruit we produce is the lives of those we witness to and lead into the kingdom. We can evangelize the world and, through the power of God in our lives, set the captives free: *"When He ascended on high, He led captivity captive, and gave gifts to men"* (Ephesians 4:8). Jesus not only led captivity captive but because He had no sin in Him, He also led sin captive. As a Christian, sin and death can no longer rule you because He arose from the dead. His righteousness and sanctification are part of the gifts God has imparted to you. Now when the Father looks at you, He sees Jesus.

One of Christ's promises was that He would come again to receive us unto Himself. He is the first of many brethren, and the things He did, we will also do. So, if He ascended into heaven, then you're going to ascend as well. Because he went up to prepare a place for you, He's coming back to take you home. Isn't that exciting? You have the best days ahead of you!

Who Am I?

Then God said, "Let Us make man in
Our image, according to Our likeness…"
(GENESIS 1:26)

"Who am I?" "Where do I fit in?" If you are a born-again Christian, you can relax, knowing that God made you and is keenly aware of every detail about you. In God's great plan, a special place was designed just for you! Yes, God has a unique calling that only you can fulfill; therefore, it's vital that you recognize His image of you and strive to fulfill that image.

The first and most important thing the Bible says about our image appears in Genesis 1:26: *"Then God said, 'Let Us make man in Our image,*

according to Our likeness.'" God wants you to fulfill every facet of your identity and to accomplish all that you set your hand to do, just as He does.

Romans 8:29 echoes this theme: *"For whom He foreknew, He also predestined to be conformed to the image of His Son."* How exciting it is to know that God considers your image to be just as beautiful as the image of Jesus Christ. The only way to fulfill your perfect place in His kingdom is to be conformed totally to the image of Jesus Christ. There is no higher calling!

Yet, some Christians don't resemble Him at all. One reason is that they are trying to imitate someone else's image. It's okay to admire other people, but it's wrong to assume that your ministry call is the same as theirs. People get "out of image" by trying to achieve something that God never called them to do. Each of us needs to discover our personal image in Him. Paul explained how this is accomplished in 2 Corinthians 3:18: *"But we all, with unveiled face, beholding as in a mirror the glory of the Lord, are being transformed into the same image from glory to glory, just as by the Spirit of the Lord."*

When you behold the glory of God, His glory becomes a part of you— and His image for you is to go from glory to glory in whatever He has called you to do. The day you received Jesus Christ as your personal Savior, you were recreated into God's image, and when you behold your true image, you begin to take on the appearance of God Himself! By beholding Him, you grow more glorious every day.

Whatever He has called you to do, I guarantee you will never be totally satisfied until you are moving in the glory of that image. God wants you to be the best at what He has called you to achieve. He is the only One who can complete your personal image. Romans 12:2 tells you how to walk in the fullness of God's image for you: *"And do not be conformed to this world, but be transformed by the renewing of your mind, that you may prove what is that good and acceptable and perfect will of God."* If you behold the Father's image, you will prove what the good, acceptable, and perfect will of God for your image is.

God's Word is the mirror of all that He has for you. When you look into the mirror and see Him, your spirit says, "That is my image." When you behold His face and fulfill His image for you, God's perfect plan for your life will go from glory to glory!

Renewal

*Create in me a clean heart, O God, and
renew a steadfast spirit within me.*

(PSALM 51:10)

The story of Samson shows us that we are made in the image of God, even if we blow it. Samson was born as a result of the prayers and faith of his parents; he was dedicated as a Nazarite (see Judges 13:5). He was raised in a godly home, was blessed, and the Spirit was in him. But his is a somewhat bizarre story. I have to wonder how God could choose him. Despite his failures and moral decline, Samson was able to fulfill the purpose that God had for him—that of a judge and deliverer—because he finally woke up and his image of himself was renewed.

In Hebrew, the word "renew" has four different meanings. The first one is to "change," as in "change for the better."

At the end of his life, after he was imprisoned by the Philistines, Samson was dragged into a Philistine gathering at their local temple. He was placed between two supporting pillars under a huge balcony where a multitude of guests had gathered. He remembered who he was and who God was, and he prayed for a final renewal: *"O Lord God, remember me, I pray! Strengthen me, I pray, just this once, O God, that I may with one blow take vengeance on the Philistines for my two eyes!"* (Judges 16:28).

When he used the word "Lord," he acknowledged God as his master. We need to behold God as master in our own lives. When Samson said, "O Lord God," he was repenting. Psalm 51:10 says, *"Create in me a clean heart, O God, and renew a steadfast spirit within me."* A clean heart means a renewed spirit. Don't hide your sin—take it to God. Behold His face and let Him renew your image.

The second meaning of "renew" is to "grow up." In this case, it implies "make young, strengthen." When Samson repented, he strengthened his true image. God "made young" His call on Samson's life to deliver Israel from the Philistines.

Renew also means to "go on" or "go forward." Samson said, "I am a deliverer," and God empowered Samson with supernatural strength to "go forward" in his image. As a result of his final prayer, Samson's strength was renewed. When he pushed against the two pillars that were supporting the temple, the whole building came crashing down on all who had gathered, killing more Philistines in his death than he had killed in his life.

The fourth meaning of renew is "to sprout again"; this is the idea of "regeneration." In this scenario, Samson was placed back into God's image for him. Samson was more glorious in his latter image than in his former image. He is even in the Hebrew "Hall of Faith" (see Hebrews 11:32).

Samson changed his ways, was renewed, and beheld his Father's face again. Similarly, no matter how dark your circumstances, God wants to restore you and make your image glorious again! When you behold Him and fulfill His image for you, God's perfect plan for your life will sprout again, and you can go from glory to glory!

Your Personal Trainer

*"My son, do not despise the chastening of the
LORD, nor be discouraged when you are rebuked
by Him; for whom the LORD loves He chastens,
and scourges every son whom He receives."*

(HEBREWS 12:5–6)

One day I asked the Lord, "What do Christians need to know to come out triumphantly when they go through tests and trials?" The Lord had me turn to Hebrews 12:5–6, *"My son, do not despise the chastening of the LORD, nor be discouraged when you are rebuked by Him; for whom the LORD loves He chastens, and scourges every son whom He receives."*
I began to see some truths that were comforting concerning the matter of God's chastening. I found out that chastening means "child training, instruction, being educated." What a difference that makes!

Every Christian will experience trials, temptations, infirmities, and afflictions, but God has promised that His personal training can cause you to win over them

all. To triumph over tests and trials, we must understand that God uses them as training grounds to help us win *"the race that is set before us"* (Hebrews 12:1). The Christian life is like a race with hurdles and obstacles to overcome. A hill or two may test our endurance and stretch our faith. If we are going to run and finish the race, then we will have to lay aside some weights (sin) that can slow us down and eventually lead to defeat (see Hebrews 12:1). We can't finish the course God has set before us if we allow sin to distract us from running the course.

Often, when we are confronted with a test, trial, or temptation, we think God is mad at us, but He isn't! There are two wrong ways to respond to God's training, found in Hebrews 12:5–6: you can *despise* God's training, and you can be discouraged and *despair* of it. When you despise the Lord's chastening, you treat it lightly. If you have bitterness, covetousness, or bad habits and the Lord uses a person or a situation to deal with it, you might say, "Well, so-and-so gets away with it, so why can't I?" If you ignore God's chastening, you are treating it lightly and could end up out of the race.

Another wrong way to respond is to despair of God's training. The Lord may put His hand on you and say, "I don't like this thing (weight) in your life; it keeps you from being victorious." You can accept God's dealing and act on His words; or you can say, "Oh, God, I just can't help it. I've tried and tried to overcome it, and I just can't. It's hopeless." But it's not hopeless! Remember: *"For whom the LORD loves He chastens, and scourges every son whom He receives"* (Hebrews 12:6). Don't faint or despair over your situation; rather, know that God's wonderful hand of love is behind it.

Training brings profit into your life. If you refuse to allow the Lord to train and discipline you, you won't mature in your Christian faith. If you despise God's training or despair in the middle of a trial, then your spiritual growth stagnates, and you are no longer of any profit to God's kingdom. How tragic! The Lord wants us to be constant producers who grow to maturity in Him because maturity leads to fruit-bearing. The Lord's chastening will yield *"the peaceable fruit of righteousness to those who have been trained by it"* (Hebrews 12:11).

Tests and trials are opportunities for spiritual exercise that strengthens our inner man and gets us ready for bigger and better things from God. The more we exercise in the spiritual realm, the more we are equipped to enter into spiritual warfare for ourselves, our loved ones, and the unsaved all around us. So, embark on God's personal training program today!

A Touch from the Master's Hands

"The altar will be most holy, and whatever touches it will be holy."

(EXODUS 29:37 NIV)

In Michelangelo's famous mural of creation on the ceiling of the Sistine Chapel, we see God reaching way down, exerting great effort to touch Adam. In the same way, God is reaching way down to touch you! He loves you so much that He wants to touch you. If you allow Him, God will touch you every day, wherever you are. The secret to receiving His touch

is captured in Michelangelo's mural, which shows God leaning, straining, and stretching to touch Adam. As you reach toward Him, know that God is already reaching toward you!

Christians need God's touch and should expect Him to touch them every day! Plus, God wants a personal touch from you! He wants to feel your presence. The awesomeness of God is such that, as you seek to reach up to Him, He reaches down and touches you with His love and compassion, just like Jesus did for the woman with the issue of blood. When she reached out and touched the hem of His garment in faith, she was healed (see Mark 5:25–34).

Touch is important because it has to do with the law of transference. In the Old Testament, when a lamb was sacrificed, the people transferred their sins onto the lamb that would die in their place. When Jesus died for us, our sins were transferred to Him. So, instead of touching us with a hand of wrath, God now transfers His anointing to set us completely free with a gentle stroke of His hand.

There is also a negative side to touch. In the Old Testament, God commanded the Israelites not to touch certain animals and things. In Genesis 2, God told Adam and Eve not to eat of the

Tree of Knowledge of Good and Evil. When they chose to dis-obey God, sin and physical death were transferred to humanity. When the Israelites were gathered at Mount Sinai, God told the people, "Don't touch the mountain!" If they or even their ani-mals did, they would die (see Exodus 19:12). He didn't want them to come near for their protection; they were unholy, and the most Holy God was residing on the mountain. Holiness cannot tolerate the transference of unholiness. If we touch and handle with affection the things of the world, their nature will transfer to us.

The blood sacrifice of the law was a way for God to touch those He loved. When the Israelites touched the head of their sacrificial lamb to transfer their sins to it and placed it on the

altar, God reached back and touched their hearts. Today, the blood of Jesus that covers believers makes it possible for God to reach way down and touch you.

If you place your heart (your sacrifice) on God's altar, He will touch you. This is how to live a holy life, for whatever touches the altar becomes holy: *"The altar will be most holy, and whatever touches it will be holy"* (Exodus 29:37 NIV). Paul urges us in Romans 12:1 to *"present your bodies a living sacrifice, holy, acceptable to God, which is your reasonable service."* Any time you put yourself on the altar, God wants to touch you, make you whole, and transfer to you what you need to become a better, happier, healthier, wealthier, and more effective Christian.

As you touch God, purpose in your heart not to let anything hinder you as you reach out in faith to Him—just like the woman with the issue of blood did. Reach out and touch Him!

Holiness

Be Holy

"Be holy, for I am holy."

(1 PETER 1:16)

Because God is holy, He wants His people to live holy lives: *"Be holy, for I am holy"* (1 Peter 1:16). But what is holiness? Holiness is simply living in the new nature God gave you when you became born-again. No matter what your past sins have been, God has a divine plan for you to live in holiness every day of your life. Your decision to walk in holiness will not only transform your life but can be instrumental in the transformation of other people's lives as well.

During one of the most tumultuous periods in his life, David learned to walk in holiness. Through his example, we find four simple keys to obtaining holiness in our lives.

David had been involved in adultery and murder, and Bathsheba had become pregnant with his baby. In order to hide his sin, David had her husband, Uriah, killed so he could marry her. The prophet Nathan went to David to expose his sins and reveal God's judgment—that someone from David's own house would take his wives, and his son would die (2 Samuel 12:11–12, 14).

David could have said, "Nathan, I am the king, and no one speaks to me like that!" But David didn't. Instead, he said to Nathan, *"I have sinned against the LORD"* (2 Samuel 12:13). That's the first key to holiness—**allow God to deal with your heart**. We must not try to cover up our sins. In order to walk in holiness, we must allow the Lord to deal with our hearts. The Lord may deal with you privately, or He may send another Christian to speak to you. Don't get caught up in *how* the Lord deals with your heart—just allow Him to do so.

How did David deal with the sins that Nathan exposed, and how did he learn to be holy? David didn't blame Bathsheba. Rather, in Psalm 51:2–3, David acknowledged his sins and took responsibility for them: *"Wash me thoroughly from my iniquity, and cleanse me from my sin. For I acknowledge my transgressions, and my sin is always before me."*

Sin is a reality in our lives, but there's a remedy for sin found in 1 John 1:9, *"If we confess our sins, He is faithful and just to forgive us our sins and to cleanse us from all unrighteousness."* That's the second key to be holy—you must do as David did; **acknowledge your sin and confess it to the Lord**. Repent and allow God to erase your sins and learn to walk in holiness.

We find the third key when David appealed to God's mercy twice in Psalm 51:1, *"Have mercy upon me, O God, according to Your lovingkindness; according to the multitude of Your tender mercies, blot out my transgressions."* We need to **appeal to God's mercy** when we have sinned. God's mercy endures forever. People who know the Lord can turn to Him for mercy. We need only ask, and He will cleanse us from our sin and make us whiter than snow (see verse 7).

The last key to holiness is found in Psalm 51:10, *"Create in me a clean heart, O God, and renew a steadfast spirit within me."* The word "create" is the same Hebrew word used in Genesis 1:1 when God "created" the heavens and the earth out of nothing. David knew that God could make something out of nothing, so he asked the Lord to create a new heart in him. **Ask the Lord to create a new heart in you.** He created a new heart in David, and He will create a new heart in you, too, because God wants to transform your life and see you walking in holiness.

Be-Attitudes

"Blessed are those who hunger and thirst for righteousness, for they shall be filled. Blessed are the merciful, for they shall obtain mercy. Blessed are the pure in heart, for they shall see God."

(MATTHEW 5:6–8)

As Christians, we often concentrate so heavily on what we can get and need from Jesus that we forget to *focus on Jesus*. We get so wrapped up in the cares of this world that we lose sight of our goal—to be like Jesus. Paul said that his number one goal was to know Jesus. Paul understood that when Christians know Jesus, they become like Him; and when they learn how to be like Jesus, then they can do the things that He did. I call this lifestyle motivation the "Be-Attitudes."

In Matthew 5, there are nine "be-attitudes," which break into three sets of three. Within each set, there is a "thesis" (a major truth), an "antithesis" (an opposite truth), and a combination of the two, or a "synthesis." For example, if hydrogen is the thesis and oxygen is the antithesis, the synthesis of the two is water.

The "be-attitude," in verse 6 explains that to be Christlike, we need to hunger and thirst after Jesus: *"Blessed are those who hunger and thirst for righteousness, for they shall be filled."* This is our "thesis." Hunger and thirst are two basic needs of life because they are intrinsically linked to self-preservation. But do you see what Jesus said here? He is telling you to use these survival instincts to seek Him through righteousness. You must become attached to the source of life—the tree of righteousness—not to the things of this world. Then, you will be filled; you will receive His kind of right thinking, right acting, and right speaking. However, you must be careful not to become so righteousness-conscious that you become legalistic.

That's why Jesus added the antithesis in verse 7: *"Blessed are the merciful, for they shall obtain mercy."* Mercy says, "If you blow it all, I'll love you anyway." God wants us to be righteous, but He wants us to be merciful, too. Jesus loves you just the way you are! That's mercy! But to major on mercy can be dangerous because if you are only merciful, then you will be a pushover. You must temper mercy and righteousness together.

So that leads to the "synthesis." Verse 8 says, *"Blessed are the pure in heart, for they shall see God."* To become so like God that you can see Him, you need to combine righteousness and mercy in your life so you can have a pure heart. When your heart is pure, you will see God in your circumstances.

There's something else interesting about mercy and righteousness. Psalm 85:10 says: *"Mercy and truth have met together; righteousness and peace have kissed."* Mercy and truth

go together, and righteousness and peace go together. I believe this refers to the mercy seat. If you recall, there were two cherubim whose wings overshadowed the mercy seat. This was the place where mercy and truth abounded and righteousness and peace came together, foreshadowing the coming Prince of Peace—and when these meet, they are in the presence of God.

Where do you experience the presence of God? Where do you see Him? When righteousness and mercy "kiss each other" in your life. That describes the Christian life.

Don't Be a Yo-Yo Christian!

*But let him ask [for wisdom] in faith, with no
doubting, for he who doubts is like a wave of
the sea driven and tossed by the wind. . . . he is a
double-minded man, unstable in all his ways.*

(JAMES 1:6, 8)

"**I** feel like a yo-yo Christian," wrote one of my readers.
"One day I'm up, and the next day I'm down." He's not
alone. Yo-yo Christians are believers who waver between
winning today and losing tomorrow. On the other hand, consecrated Christians overcome defeat by getting a strong grip on
God and letting Him pull them through every situation.

Lot was a yo-yo believer. Even though the Bible
calls him a righteous man, Lot's level of consecration was at ground zero! He was what
James 1:8 calls *"a double-minded man,
unstable in all his ways."* One consequence of being a yo-yo Christian

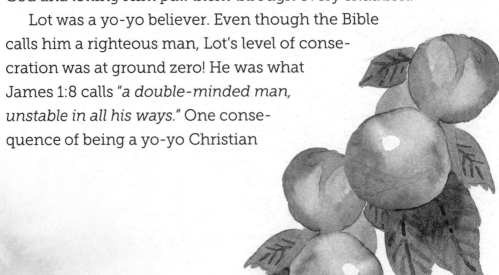

is the likelihood of making foolish choices. Lot's troubles began when he foolishly chose to do his own thing rather than follow the godly leadership of Abram.

When Lot moved to Sodom, he *"was oppressed by the filthy conduct of the wicked"* (2 Peter 2:7). I believe the vulgar lifestyle of the Sodomites further eroded Lot's consecration. Similarly, the current culture in America is also eroding many Christians' consecration. Look at Lot's reaction when the Sodomites demanded that he hand over God's angels. Did Lot say, "God, these are your angels, I trust you to protect us all from evil"? No! Lot was on the downswing of the yo-yo; and although he may have been spiritual enough to know that he was entertaining angels, Lot didn't trust God's provision for the situation. Instead, he acted out of his own reasoning and tried to bargain with the mob (see Genesis 19).

Yo-yo Christians soon lose the ability to discern spiritual things. Do you remember what happened in Genesis 14 when Lot was taken hostage by Chedorlaomer's army? Lot had no spiritual discernment. He couldn't see that God wanted to use this hostage situation as an opportunity to move Lot and his family back to Canaan. So, when Abram and his army of 318 servants pursued Chedorlaomer, defeated him, and rescued the hostages, Lot took his family right back to Sodom.

Yo-yo Christians make all kinds of excuses for their carnal behavior; drinking alcoholic beverages certainly compounded Lot's misery (see Genesis 19:32–38). Mentally and emotionally, Lot was probably at his lowest ebb. Driven from Sodom, he may have had a pity party, "Oh, poor me! I have lost every-thing: my lovely wife, my position at the gate of the city, my beautiful home with the two-donkey garage. One drink won't hurt!" So, Lot took a drink. In fact, Lot got drunk; and while he was in a drunken stupor, his daughters committed incest with him. Yuck!

Although Lot knew God, his relationship with God had become distant and cold. This condition is present in many believers' lives today. They may love God, but they have failed to wholly consecrate their lives and enter into an intimate rela-tionship with Him. If that describes you, tomorrow we will look at how you can consecrate yourself and be set free from the yo-yo syndrome. For now, prepare for your consecration and pray with me:

> Dear Lord, I'm tired of living a yo-yo life.
> I repent of my unstable ways and want
> to be a consecrated Christian. I believe
> you will guide me and correct me in all
> my ways, so that I can be a righteous
> Christian. In Jesus's name, amen.

Becoming a Consecrated Christian

"You shall anoint them, consecrate them, and sanctify them, that they may minister to Me as priests."

(EXODUS 28:41)

Powerful ministries flow from a person who has wholly consecrated him or herself to God. You would not believe the level of consecration that Chinese Christians have! On a mission trip to China, I heard a man's testimony that really gave a new twist to the concept of "prison ministry." Because of his commitment to Christ, he was sentenced to prison for five years. Upon his arrival, he began to seek God through fasting and prayer. Soon, other prisoners were saved and joined him in prayer for the guards, who subsequently became Christians. When one of them was given a Bible, they began to meet in the courtyard. The newly converted guards would even look the other way, allowing some prisoners to slip out at night to preach the gospel in the surrounding villages. That "prison ministry" started many underground churches that remain strong today.

A ministry this powerful doesn't flow from the life of a yo-yo Christian. It flows from a person who has wholly consecrated themselves to God.

God commanded the Israelites to make burnt offerings, often for consecration—God's solution for ending the yo-yo syndrome. God told Moses to consecrate Aaron and his sons: *"You shall anoint them, consecrate them, and sanctify them, that they may minister to Me as priests"* (Exodus 28:41). Aaron had been a yo-yo believer—remember, he built the golden calf! After his consecration, you see a man who really took on a godly leadership role in the community.

As Christians, we are also part of a royal priesthood: *"But you are a chosen generation, a royal priesthood, . . . that you may proclaim the praises of Him who called you out of darkness into His marvelous light"* (1 Peter 2:9). We have been consecrated by the blood of Jesus. However, if you want to *wholly* consecrate yourself to God, there are several steps you can take to change your life.

1. The decision to consecrate yourself to God must be made voluntarily and is probably the wisest choice you'll ever make. The man in China certainly could have become bitter and rebellious—as many do when they are persecuted for the sake of righteousness. However, this man made the wise choice to seek God's provision for his situation through fasting and prayer.

2. Consecration involves trusting God. Someone once said to me, "Marilyn, my finances are so tight; I just can't afford to tithe." I responded, "You can't afford *not* to tithe." Folks, if you can trust God with your eternal destiny, certainly you can trust Him concerning your finances.

3. No matter how busy you are, make the sacrifice to spend at least one hour every day seeking God through prayer and Bible reading to gain spiritual discernment. Then, by faith, exercise that spiritual discernment in all the decisions you make throughout the day.

4. To stop the up-and-down life, you must stop making excuses for your carnal behavior. Instead, confess your sins to God, *"If we confess our sins, he is faithful and just to forgive us our sins and to cleanse us from all unrighteousness"* (1 John 1:9). God will forgive you and cleanse you from the thing that caused you to fall away from Him in the first place.

Allow God to forgive and restore you to that very special place of intimate consecration in Him and set you free from the yo-yo syndrome once and for all!

God's Word Covers It

For the Word of the LORD is right and
true; he is faithful in all he does.

(PSALM 33:4 NIV)

After nearly 50 years of ministry, I've seen people face situations you can't imagine and challenges that would try the hardiest of souls armed with nothing more than the Word of God. Despite seemingly impossible odds, God's Word prevailed. My commitment to teaching the Word is the foundation upon which my life and ministry are built. My message has never changed. God's Word is still the key to success, happiness, health, and victory.

Life is brimming with challenges. Sometimes things turn out as we'd hoped; sometimes they don't. Either way, a strong foundation will keep us standing. That kind of security can only come through a real relationship with God and His Word. The two are inseparable—and we need both!

Do you have questions? God's Word covers it! We'd all like to have a ready answer for every situation. As a Christian leader, I'm often asked tough questions like, "If God loves me, why did this tragedy happen?" or, "If I'm a good person, how did I get into this mess?" When we don't have the answers, we need to know where to go for *the* answer: God's Word. It alone provides the unfailing truth we need to avoid detours, confusion, and heartache.

God's Word not only solves life's mysteries, it also gives us a godly perspective. As the Word takes a preeminent position in your life, you will be able to maintain a clear picture of the issues confronting you and your loved ones. That kind of clarity helps you see what's really important. When you understand what really matters, you won't feel pressured by "little" things. Rest assured that God knows what you need and cares about everything that concerns you—even before you ask for His help.

Strong, intimate relationships require attention and care; the deeper the commitment, the deeper the relationship. The same is true with God. When you approach the Bible (His Word) from a relational perspective, it will revolutionize the way you see the Scriptures. Instead of words on a page, it will become truth in your heart. When you are open and responsive to what He says, you can develop the fulfilling relationship with God that you've always wanted.

A relationship with God and His Word is empowering. As you apply His truth to your life, you'll find your questions answered, your perspectives clarified, and your fears dissolved. As you go a step further and say what His Word says, you'll see negative situations change for the better. You'll experience healing in your body, finances, and relationships, and you'll begin to see victory at every turn. When challenges arise, you won't feel weak or inadequate—because you'll know that since you are armed with His Word, you can be victorious!

During an average day, you probably find yourself called upon to fulfill a variety of roles. Each role carries unique demands and can stretch you beyond your natural abilities. That's when you need the supernatural strength, power, and encouragement found only in the Bible. The strong foundation of God's Word enables you to grow because it keeps you in an intimate relationship with Him. There is incredible peace knowing that we can always depend upon what He says and on His love for us. It is through His Word that we have access to the success, happiness, health, and victory that are ours in Christ. So, cover your life with the Word of God.

Receive Your Miracle

*"Is there no prophet of the Lord here, that
we may inquire of the Lord by him?"*
(2 KINGS 3:11)

*H*ave you ever thought that it's easier to believe God will
work a miracle for someone else than to believe He'll work
one for you? You are not alone! Fortunately, with God, there is
no such thing as a "hopeless" situation. Our Father God spe-
cializes in "impossible" situations and delights in giving us
miracles. All we need to know is how to receive them!

Look at 2 Kings 3 to find out how you can receive your miracle. The story is of two kings: ungodly Jehoram, the king of the
ten tribes of Israel; and godly Jehoshaphat, the king of the two
tribes of Judah. Jehoshaphat served God with all his heart and
led his kingdom to do likewise.

Every year, King Jehoram received 100,000 lambs and the
wool from 100,000 rams from the king of Moab. For 150 years,
Moab had paid tribute to Israel—since the time David conquered Moab (see 2 Samuel 8:2). But after 150 years, Mesha,
the current king of Moab, decided to stop paying it.
King Jehoram was deeply concerned over

this loss to Israel's economy, so he asked Jehoshaphat for help (see 2 Kings 3:7). Jehoshaphat should not have been helping an ungodly king fight his battles! In his desire for peace, he didn't do what God really wanted him to do; he compromised.

Jehoram also made an alliance with the king of Edom, and the three kings prepared to go to war with Moab (v. 9). While on their way to Moab, the army ran out of water, and it looked like God was against them. King Jehoshaphat wanted a word from the Lord. *"Is there no prophet of the LORD here, that we may inquire of the LORD by him?"* (v. 11). When they heard that Elisha was there, they went to him, who ignored the idolatrous Jehoram but honored Jehoshaphat and prayed. God answered his prayer and told them what to do to prepare to receive their miracle—dig ditches in the valley (vv. 14–18).

When you ask the Lord for a miracle, He will usually give you something to do. This is your part to play in the miracle—an opportunity to put your faith into action. The word Elisha gave to the kings required action on their part. I have found that God usually asks something practical—our obedience to His command causes the miracles to come. If you say, "I'm too busy to follow God's lead," then you'll miss your miracle. The kings and their armies did as they were told, but nothing happened right away. Watch it—there is a testing time after you do the will of God before you see your miracle. Their miracle didn't come on the same day—it came the next morning when the grain offering was offered (v. 20). The valley was miraculously filled with water.

God has a miracle for every crisis. When you hit a crisis, you need to call on the Lord. He alone has a sure word of wisdom for your situation and can set the stage for you to receive your miracle. However, God has a part for you to play and a time of testing. So, what is God's timing for your miracle? Jesus purchased every miracle you could ever need 2,000 years ago. All you need to do is ask: "Father, in Jesus's name, I need my miracle!" Then do what He tells you to do. Stand in faith during the time of testing, and you can receive your miracle.

Midnight-Hour Anointing

And the yoke will be destroyed
because of the anointing oil.

(ISAIAH 10:27)

Are you facing a midnight hour in some area of your life? Are things looking darker than ever before? Are you (or a loved one) confronted with a midnight hour in your health, job, or finances? Is the clock striking midnight on a bill, loan, job search, or family struggle? If you or someone you love is facing a midnight hour, then read the following carefully—because midnight hours are often life or death, make-it or break-it, do-or-die situations.

The Holy Spirit directed me to look at every recorded midnight situation in the Bible.

Without fail, when people obeyed God, their midnight hours became miracle turning points of divine intervention, deliverance, and destiny. For example:

- In Exodus 12, the Israelites' firstborns were delivered from death at midnight.
- In Judges 16, God caused Samson to rise at midnight and carry off the city gates, leading to the deliverance of God's children.
- In Ruth 3, Ruth was obedient to the Lord's leading as she lay at the feet of Boaz at midnight, and the lineage of Jesus was preserved.
- In Acts 16, Paul and Silas were singing praises to God at midnight in jail, and the other prisoners heard them. Following the earthquake, Paul and Silas were freed, and the jailer and his family were saved.

In the Old Testament, when the Israelites were passed over by the death angel, I don't think they sat in fear; they were protected by the blood on their doorposts. I think they sat in the anointing of what God was doing. Why? Because the only thing that can pass through the blood is the anointing. The devil can't go through the blood—it stops him dead in his tracks. But the anointing can always pass through the blood. Look at when Aaron and his sons were anointed. The blood of the

consecrated lamb was put on their right ears, thumbs, and big toes (see Leviticus 8:23). The blood preceded the anointing, and the anointing is for God's people.

In the New Testament, the outpouring of the Holy Spirit and the anointing didn't come until after the cross and crucifixion. The anointing couldn't come without the blood, for it must come through the blood. If you want to move into the future with an anointing, you can because the blood of Jesus makes a way for you. If you choose the blood and the anointing of the Holy Spirit, then you can destroy the yokes of the enemy: *"And the yoke will be destroyed because of the anointing oil"* (Isaiah 10:27). By destroying the works of the enemy, your life takes on a whole new meaning and perspective—you become a conqueror!

People watch what you do in the midnight hour situations of your life. They take note of how you respond to your darkest times and deepest challenges. Unsaved loved ones watch how you handle a crisis. Paul and Silas could have whined and complained; but, with the prisoners listening, they continued to worship and celebrate Jesus, the Light of the World, in their darkest hour. God has a miracle for your midnight hour. Whether it comes in the form of divine intervention or miracles of deliverance, it will come because you have the anointing. It will soon be your turn to rejoice!

Your Custom-Made Miracle

*"Sir, give me this water, that I may not
thirst, nor come here to draw."*
(JOHN 4:15)

When we look at God's Word, it's easy to see that it is His plan to take something that everyone thinks is hopeless and make it very special! God loves to get His hands on our most desperate situations and create "custom-made" miracles to solve them. Some of the most influential people in the Bible started out as miserable people in hopeless situations—until God gave them a custom-made miracle!

Because they had intermarried with Gentiles, the Samaritans were hopeless outcasts to the Jews—until Jesus got ahold of them. Jesus decided to go through Samaria (see John 4:4). Why? Because that is where the hopeless outcasts lived. *"So He came to a city of Samaria which is called Sychar"* (John 4:5). There, at noon, a woman came to the well, and Jesus asked her for a drink. This was unusual because Jews did not speak to Samaritans. In addition, she was obviously a loose woman in a hopeless situation—only outcast Samaritans came to the well in the heat of high noon. But Jesus had a custom-made miracle waiting for her. Just as He always reaches out to us, Jesus took the initiative to reach out to this woman.

Jesus didn't care about her reputation or His. He *"made Himself of no reputation"* (see Philippians 2:7) so that He could create a miracle to bring her out of her hopeless situation. He met the woman on her own ground and essentially offered her a wonderful gift. God never forces anyone to receive His gifts. When Jesus said that He would give the Samaritan woman living water, He was wooing her to ask for the gift. And she asked, *"Sir, give me this water, that I may not thirst, nor come here to draw"* (John 4:15).

Too many times, we get off track by looking at our seemingly hopeless circumstances. We can't imagine how God can save us from the mess we've created. But Jesus guides us by saying, "Focus your attention on me and the gift that I have for you. I have a custom-made miracle for you if you have faith in me."

Before we can receive our custom-made miracle, we must first get right with God. After the woman asked for Jesus's living water, He didn't simply give it to her. He first dealt with her sin. Jesus told her to bring her husband, even though He knew she wasn't married. *"'Go, call your husband, and come here.' The woman answered and said, 'I have no husband'"* (John 4:16–17). First, He wanted to deal with her conscience. Then He dealt with her heart by saying, *"and come here."* He was saying, "You've sinned, but I still love you. Return to me. Then I will give you a well."

When Jesus told the woman that He was the Messiah, she left her waterpot behind. Immediately, she ran into the city to share her miracle with the men of the city. She shared the well of living water that was springing up so high that it was watering others! I believe she planted many seeds in Samaria by her witness and perhaps even helped to prepare it for what was to come—Samaria became one of the major centers of Christianity in the early church! (See Acts 8:14–15.)

If you ever feel hopeless or feel that your well isn't flowing, then follow the example of the Samaritan woman—let Jesus create a custom-made miracle for your situation.

There's a Miracle in That Mess

*For our light affliction, which is but for
a moment, is working for us a far more
exceeding and eternal weight of glory.*

(2 CORINTHIANS 4:17)

Are you having problems with your job, your finances, or a relationship? Are you suffering from an illness? Is your heart aching for a loved one who is far from God? Could you summarize the situation by saying, "My life, or the life of someone I love, is a muddled mess!"? The good news is that your mess can be God's means to bring a miraculous blessing into your life.

Your situation may seem overwhelming, but in every mess a Christian encounters, there is a miracle in the making. Most of the time, we look at trouble as something bad. But when we overcome a difficult situation through God's grace and power, our victory is an opportunity to receive glory (greater blessings) and give glory (praise and thanks) to God. We also have the great privilege of reflecting His glory. A little trouble can yield a heap of glory.

God says your afflictions are light compared to the heavy blessings they can bring into your life: *"For our light affliction, which is but for a moment, is working for us a far more exceeding and eternal weight of glory"* (2 Corinthians 4:17). Who in the natural would think that financial problems, sickness, or any other difficulty could be a benefit? But in God's supernatural world, afflictions can lead to glory. God wants to use the very thing the devil works against you to bring glory into your life.

God has a process to bring His glory into your life; if you grasp the process, you'll receive the glory. The way we handle hard times and deal with difficult moments provides a foundation upon which God builds a beautiful life. Joseph is a good example of someone who grasped this process. God turned a mess into a miracle in Joseph's life, and He can work a wonder in yours, too. So, let's look at how you can get God's glory in your situation. Consider these four keys.

1. Focus on the Word of God: *"While we do not look at the things which are seen, but at the things which are not seen. For the things which are seen are temporary, but the things which are not seen are eternal"* (2 Corinthians 4:18). Look at what God says about you and your problems. No matter what others say or how things look in the natural, look at the invisible.

2. Confess the Word. Don't just read the Word—speak it, confessing the invisible. If you have spoken negatively into your situation, ask for forgiveness and begin to speak positive, Bible-backed confessions.

3. Have patience and faith. Hebrews 6:12 says that it is through faith and patience that we inherit the promises of God. Patiently walk by faith. Some people want their glory now. They don't want to wait, but God needs to work on us first to prepare us for the glory to come.

4. Take hold of joy. While you are waiting for your victory, *"Do not sorrow, for the joy of the LORD is your strength"* (Nehemiah 8:10). Look at your mess the way Jesus looked upon His excruciating death on the cross as the means to a miracle: *"For the joy that was set before Him endured the cross…"* (Hebrews 12:2).

When problems arise, focus on and confess God's Word. Walk in faith and patience while you take hold of joy. Your mess is merely the means to your miracle. Your glory is on the way!

The Grace Advantage

*Bearing with one another, and forgiving one another,
if anyone has a complaint against another; even
as Christ forgave you, so you also must do.*

(COLOSSIANS 3:13)

After the fall, God could have sought revenge for Adam and Eve's disobedience. Instead, God promised to send His only Son to be an offering for sins. Grace, in this instance, involved the shedding of blood for the forgiveness of sin to restore man's fellowship with His Creator.

Because God extended grace, both sides benefitted: God and man received an increase over what each possessed originally. God not only received back his Son from the dead, but Jesus was also *"The firstborn among many*

brethren" (Romans 8:29). God got an increase on His sacrifice—He got the church! You may not think you're an advantage to God, but He thinks you are worth the price of Jesus's death! Throughout the centuries, every person who has been born-again is God's increase.

You benefitted too. When Adam and Eve sinned, they lost the garden of Eden, but the meek will inherit the earth (Matthew 5:5). They lived in Eden, but you sit together in heavenly places with Christ Jesus (Ephesians 2:6). Adam was given dominion to subdue and conquer the earth, but you are more than a conqueror through Christ (Romans 8:37). God always wants to give you more than you had before.

So, how do you treat others when you are wronged? Is seeking revenge the first thing that pops into your mind? The Bible teaches the principle of extending grace in order to turn your disadvantage into an advantage. But first, you need to cast that irritation on the Lord: *"Casting all your care upon Him, for He cares for you"* (1 Peter 5:7). Regardless of what the person did to you, the Word tells us to forgive one another, *"Bearing with one another, and forgiving one another, if anyone has a complaint against another; even as Christ forgave you, so you also must do"* (Colossians 3:13). The key to doing that is to recall that *Christ forgave you.*

If you are born-again, then you received grace when you were saved. You didn't deserve it, but as we have seen, Jesus gave you more than you ever had before; consequently, you're now enjoying a life of grace and blessings. We have the grace to forgive others. If you dispense that grace by forgiving others, you will end up richer.

Because God extended grace, both you and the person who offended you can benefit. So, do as the Lord did: don't seek revenge. Rather, extend grace!

Overcoming Fear
& Obstacles

The Key to Crisis Management

*By faith Noah, being divinely warned of things
not yet seen, moved with godly fear, prepared
an ark for the saving of his household, by which
he condemned the world and became heir of the
righteousness which is according to faith.*

(HEBREWS 11:7)

The period in Earth's history before the flood was the worst ever known. It was so bad that Genesis 6:11–13 tells us that God said He was going to destroy the earth and mankind. Only Noah heard Him because he *"found grace in the eyes of the LORD"* (Genesis 6:8). Noah looked to God instead of his circumstances, and God gave him the grace to overcome them. God will give you the grace to bring you through your times of crisis, too.

The key to getting through crises is looking to God first, who then gives you the grace to walk with Him. When Noah looked to God and found grace, he found that he could do what God told him to do: build the ark. As we read in Hebrews 11:7, we see that Noah acted by faith:

"By faith Noah, being divinely warned of things not yet seen, moved with godly fear, prepared an ark for the saving of his household, by which he condemned the world and became heir of the righteousness which is according to faith." The basis of that faith was the word of God. God warned men in the days prior to the flood that they were disobeying Him, but only Noah and his family heeded the warning and were saved. The basis of our faith is also the Word of God. We can share it with others, but it is up to them to accept it.

This verse tells us the **sphere of Noah's faith**: *"of things not yet seen."* Noah and his generation had never seen rain, but that didn't stop Noah from preaching that God was going to destroy the earth. In his years of preaching before the flood, he never had a single convert! No doubt he was thought a fool. When we obey God, it may cost us popularity and criticism, but in the end, faith in things not yet seen will pay off.

This verse also says that Noah was moved with fear. The **character of his faith** was such that Noah was more afraid of God than man. If you're going to walk in faith, your fear of God must outweigh your fear of man.

The **evidence of his faith** was that Noah acted on God's word and prepared an ark. There is always a result of your faith, in this case, an ark. When you obey God and faithfully stand on His Word, you can see the evidence of your faith. In Noah's case, the result of his faith became the saving of his house; without the ark, they would have perished—and we would never be here now.

Finally, Noah received the **reward of his faith**: Noah walked with God and received His righteousness (see Hebrews 11:7). Righteousness led to **worship.** After he and his family left the ark, Noah built an altar, offered sacrifices to God, and worshipped Him. Worship is a dialog with God; it's a lifestyle. As a result of his worship, *"The LORD smelled a soothing aroma. Then the LORD said in His heart, 'I will never again curse the ground for man's sake'"* (Genesis 8:21). When you worship God, the curses begin to break.

God tells us to call on Him, and He will answer. He will show us great and mighty things which we do not know. (Jeremiah 33:3). You have a direct hotline to God. All you must do is look to God and call on Him to receive His grace. God will take you through every crisis. Cry to God, who hears you and delivers you.

Fear Not!

*God has not given us a spirit of fear, but of
power and of love and of a sound mind.*

(2 TIMOTHY 1:7)

Think back to the year 2000. People were consumed by fear of the new millennium. Experts predicted a computer (and even a societal) collapse, but when 2000 rolled in, nothing happened. More recently, think about the fear that 2020 ushered in—the coronavirus held the world captive with fear. That's how fear works. While the apparent threat looms large, the effects of fear are very real. If you're not careful, life can be a roller coaster ride of emotional extremes dictated by the rise and fall of emergencies. While some emergencies warrant great concern, the spirit of fear has no place controlling our responses because, in the final analysis, we serve a big God.

When Paul was awaiting execution and Christians were being brutalized by Nero, Paul wrote to Timothy, who feared for his own life and the future of the church. Paul encouraged Timothy, saying: *"God has not given us a spirit of fear, but of power and of love and of a sound mind"* (2 Timothy 1:7). When fear keeps you in limbo, face it squarely and ask God for the grace to overcome it. Whether your fear is a deep spiritual dread or a phobia-like reaction to spiders, lightning, or crowds—fear will flee when you turn to God. We are human, and there will always be situations that frighten us. First Peter 1:6–7 says:

> *In all this you greatly rejoice, . . . you may have had*
> *to suffer grief in all kinds of trials. These have come*
> *so that the proven genuineness of your faith—*
> *of greater worth than gold, which perishes even*
> *though refined by fire—may result in praise, glory*
> *and honor when Jesus Christ is revealed.* (NIV)

Peter said we would face tests, but he knew God's grace would bring us through.

The devil uses fear to keep you from fulfilling God's call on your life. Like any attack of Satan, fear is overcome by obeying God's command to resist him (see James 4:7). Face fear and take authority over it. Command it to go in Jesus's name, and God's grace will make you victorious!

Paul compared us to soldiers, athletes, and farmers to give us tangible examples of how to win. A soldier is tough and willing to endure hardships: *"You therefore must endure hardship as a good soldier of Jesus Christ"* (2 Timothy 2:3). He might walk for miles and sleep in mud, yet he remains on guard, always ready for battle. We, too, must stay alert and keep our emotions in line with God's Word so we can neutralize the devil's arsenal of fear and stand against his schemes.

When you're afraid, your heart beats faster, your palms sweat, and you want to run, but Paul says to train yourself to win over fear. Become like an athlete who works hard, trains daily, and demands the best of himself. Take control and follow God's rules: *"If anyone competes in athletics, he is not crowned unless he competes according to the rules"* (2 Timothy 2:5).

In 2 Timothy 2:6, Paul likens the spirit of the Christian to that of a farmer, *"The hardworking farmer must be first to partake of the crops."* The farmer is the first to taste the fruit of his labors; the Christian should be first to experience the fruit of the Spirit. Be diligent and patient—plant the Word in your heart, tend it carefully, and pull up any weeds (fear, doubt, unbelief) that might choke out a good crop. When fear comes, your spirit will overflow with a harvest of power, love, and a sound mind to carry you through.

God will give you the grace and power to stand up to fear. It is up to you to call on Him for the strength to look fear in the eye, draw a line in the sand, and rest in the safety of His supernatural touch.

Your Power Source

Therefore I will boast all the more gladly about my weaknesses, so that Christ's power may rest on me. That is why, for Christ's sake, I delight in weaknesses, . . . For when I am weak, then I am strong.

(2 CORINTHIANS 12:9–10 NIV)

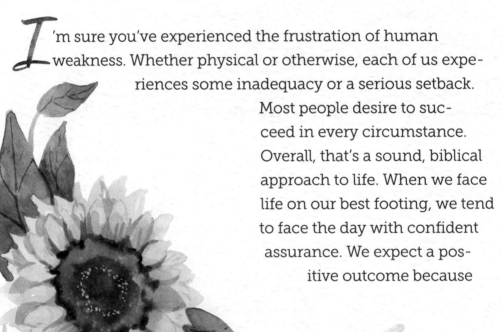

I'm sure you've experienced the frustration of human weakness. Whether physical or otherwise, each of us experiences some inadequacy or a serious setback. Most people desire to succeed in every circumstance. Overall, that's a sound, biblical approach to life. When we face life on our best footing, we tend to face the day with confident assurance. We expect a positive outcome because we've done everything right. However, when something upsets the delicate balance of "feeling in control," our true weakness becomes evident.

The good news is that, regardless of the world's wisdom or even your own past experiences, your success is not based upon your strength—and failure is not formed in your weakness. We must surrender our desire to be in control to God, giving Him total access to our lives and our weaknesses. Paul is the perfect example. Paul was well-acquainted with weakness, yet God used him to accomplish much. When a "thorn in his flesh" tormented him, he cried out to God for relief: *"Three times I pleaded with the Lord to take it away from me. But he said to me, 'My grace is sufficient for you, for my power is made perfect in weakness'"* (2 Corinthians 12:8–9 NIV).

Knowing all that God still had planned for Paul, you might think He would have removed every hindrance—especially the thorn that caused him such pain. Instead, God showed Paul a new way of looking at his weakness. God knows that man's strength can only go so far, for so long. Ultimately, our strength is insufficient. When we acknowledge that fact and turn to Him, we switch from our own "power supply" to His grace—His limitless ability exercised on our behalf.

After God's unexpected answer, the apostle gained a new perspective on weakness: *"Therefore I will boast all the more gladly about my weaknesses, so that Christ's power may rest on me. That is why, for Christ's sake, I delight in weaknesses, . . . For when I am weak, then I am strong"* (2 Corinthians 12:9–10

NIV). Instead of begging God to fix the problem, Paul boasted and delighted in it. Paul delighted in his weakened condition because he realized that with God backing Him up, every obstacle became an opportunity for God's power to be demonstrated.

Allow weakness to work for you and for the kingdom. Ask God what you can learn through periods of seeming failure, defeat, or frailty. Acknowledge God's strength. Release yourself into His hands and draw on His unending power. Even when weakness is all your natural eye can see, you can enjoy the genuine victory that comes only from God. Each deflated expectation can turn out to be your open door to accomplishment. Any challenging experience can become an equipping moment of success—when you allow God to work through your weakness.

Finally, when you're feeling weak or inadequate, remember that Jesus Himself was ridiculed as He hung on the cross (see Mark 15:32). Beaten and bloodied, He was not the world's typical picture of strength. Yet His "weakness" was used by God to bring salvation to the world!

Freedom through Forgiveness

"Whatever you bind on earth will be bound in heaven, and whatever you loose on earth will be loosed in heaven."

(MATTHEW 18:18)

*F*orgiveness is a powerful force. We can loose others with our forgiveness, or we can bind them with our unforgiveness. We can loose ourselves from torment by forgiving, or we can place ourselves in torment by not forgiving.

Do you remember the story in Matthew 18:23–34 about the man who owed the king 10,000 talents? In order to pay a debt of this size, the man, his wife, and his children would be sold into slavery. But the king had compassion and "loosed" him by forgiving his debt. How overwhelmed he must have been by the king's compassion and goodness!

Then the roles were reversed. The forgiven servant had a debtor who owed him one hundred denarii. In contrast to the benevolent king, the servant threw his debtor into debtors' prison! When the king heard of his servant's behavior, he turned the ungrateful servant over to the "torturers" until his debt was paid!

The end of this story is very sad. One man was bound in prison because of another's unforgiveness, and the unforgiving servant was tormented. We live in a very dangerous condition when we don't forgive because we, too, are living in torment. Jesus said that if we don't forgive others, the King of our lives will not forgive us: *"If you do not forgive men their trespasses, neither will your Father forgive your trespasses"* (Matthew 6:15).

When we forgive, we loose the forgiven offender. Matthew 18:18 says, *"Whatever you bind on earth will be bound in heaven, and whatever you loose on earth will be loosed in heaven."* We free the offender by our faith, because whomever we loose on earth is loosed in heaven. Heaven will begin to work on the offender, and our prayer power will increase.

We can destroy people with our unforgiveness or edify them with forgiveness, but we must make the godly decision. Jesus could have destroyed us because of our sins. Instead, His one desire was to edify us. Therefore, He forgave us! Paul said in Philippians 3:10, *"That I may know Him and the power*

of His resurrection, and the fellowship of His sufferings, being conformed to His death." If we are to know Jesus in His suffering, we must feel what He felt for those who offended Him. He wanted to die on the cross for their sins because He loved them. And He loves us too!

There is no better time to forgive than right now! Take a few moments to think of people who have offended you. Now say this prayer with me:

> Dear Father, I come to you in the name of Jesus.
> I forgive (list names here) with the love of Jesus.
> Now, by God's power, I forget the incidents
> that offended me. I command my feelings
> to line up with the Word of God. Jesus said,
> *"Therefore if the Son makes you free, you shall
> be free indeed"* (John 8:36). Thank you, Father,
> for setting me free in Jesus's name, amen.

These are powerful truths by which to live. If you allow Jesus to give you His love for your offenders, you can begin to live free. Forgiveness is the divine way of living! Forgive and live free!

Forgive and Forget

*If we confess our sins, He is faithful and just to forgive
us our sins and to cleanse us from all unrighteousness.*

(1 JOHN 1:9)

There is much more to forgiveness than the simple act of forgiving others. God's forgiveness is not a one-time experience—it is a way of living.

We experience forgiveness for all of our sins when we receive Jesus as Savior. First John 1:9 tells us, "*If we confess our sins, He is faithful and just to forgive us our sins and to cleanse us from all unrighteousness.*" There are two key aspects of God's forgiveness: (1) He freely forgives us when we confess our sins; and (2) He forgets our sins and never remembers them again. Confession and repentance are the conditions we must fulfill to be forgiven. Forgiving and forgetting our sins is God's response to our meeting those conditions.

God forgives and forgets, and He wants us to do the same. Both you and I have probably said, "I forgive, but I never forget." Forgiving and forgetting the sins of others are Siamese twins.

They can't be separated. The apostles learned this powerful truth in their walk with Jesus. Jesus told them specifically how to behave when they were offended by their brethren:

> *"Take heed to yourselves. If your brother sins against you, rebuke him; and if he repents, forgive him. And if he sins against you seven times in a day, and seven times in a day returns to you, saying, 'I repent,' you shall forgive him."* (LUKE 17:3-4)

The apostles understood that they could not act on their own emotions or according to circumstances. They had to act on Jesus's spoken words. They needed increased faith to experience increased forgiving. Hearing and acting on God's Word will increase your faith. Increased faith will give you increased power to forgive.

Joseph demonstrated the acts of forgiving and forgetting. Joseph forgave and also forgot the dastardly conduct of his brothers because he named his first child, Manasseh, which means "causing to forget." He then named his second child, Ephraim, which means "double fruit" (see Genesis 41:51–52). When we forgive and forget, we become fruitful in every area of our lives—spiritually, mentally, emotionally, and physically. We cannot find one area of Joseph's life that wasn't fruitful.

When you forgive by faith, you can claim divine power to forget by faith. It is divine to forgive, and it is also divine to forget. Too many times, we struggle to forgive by feelings when true forgiveness takes place by faith in God's Word. Like Paul, we must learn to forgive in the person of Jesus Christ (see 2 Corinthians 2:10).

Forgiveness is a powerful force. We can loose others with our forgiveness, or we can bind them with our unforgiveness. We can loose ourselves from torment by forgiving, or we can place ourselves in torment by not forgiving. By faith, allow Jesus to teach you how to love your offenders in the same way He loved and forgave you. It won't be the end of your forgiving; it will be the beginning.

Standing in the Gap

*"I sought for a man among them who would . . .
stand in the gap before Me . . . but I found no one."*
(EZEKIEL 22:30)

G od wants us to stand in the gap for others, not because they deserve it, but because Jesus died for them. Jesus took the punishment we should have received. We deserved to go to hell, but Jesus said, "I'll go for you." He stood in the gap for us. When we accept Jesus, we receive His nature and are to stand in the gap and pray for others instead of pointing a finger at them.

The book of Philemon contains one of the most outstanding messages in the Bible because it gives us a beautiful picture of Jesus, who *"took our infirmities and bore our sicknesses"* (Matthew 8:17). It also illustrates what Jesus did for us: *"Blessed is he whose transgression is forgiven, whose sin is covered. Blessed is the man to whom the LORD does not impute iniquity . . ."* (Psalm 32:1–2). To impute means "charge his account with." When we "impute" something to someone else, we give it to them, and they willingly take it from us and

carry it upon themselves. This was illustrated by Jesus at Calvary, and Paul beautifully portrays this act of imputation in the book of Philemon.

Paul wrote to Philemon about Onesimus, Philemon's slave, who had stolen from Philemon and ran away. Although Onesimus fled from his master as a sinner, he was later converted to Christianity by Paul. Paul wrote this letter on Onesimus's behalf, asking for mercy and his total restoration. Paul reminded Philemon that because Christ had forgiven him, he, too, should forgive Onesimus. Onesimus was now Paul's spiritual son and a joint heir in Christ with Philemon. Then Paul added, *"If then you count me as a partner, receive him as you would me. But if he has wronged you or owes anything, put that on my account. . . . I will repay"* (Philemon 17–19).

The end result of Paul's intercession for Onesimus was that he was forgiven and restored to Philemon. We find proof of this in Colossians 4:9, where Paul mentions Onesimus as a "faithful and beloved brother."

It's so easy to identify the gaps and expose another's shortcomings, but it's supernatural to stand in the gap and pray for them. When Paul wrote Philemon, he was painting a picture of Jesus Christ. Ezekiel 22:30 says, *"So I sought for a man among them who would . . . stand in the gap before Me . . . but I found no one."* Today, God is looking for men and women who, when they see a brother in trouble, will stand in the gap like Paul did for Onesimus and Jesus did for us.

Paul didn't gloss over Onesimus's wrongdoing and deny that he had run away from Philemon without leave. He acknowledged Onesimus was wrong, then went a step further when he said, "Impute his actions to me. I'll pay the bill." That's what happened at Calvary. Jesus said to the Father, "They have repented, and I have forgiven them. When you look at them, see me." When the Father looks at us, He sees us through the blood of Jesus Christ, who stamped our bill **"Paid In Full!"**

Perhaps you have bitterness and unforgiveness in your heart toward someone who has hurt you. If so, make a conscious decision by faith right now to forgive them and make your faith effectual by acknowledging the love of God which is in you by the Spirit of God (see Romans 5:5).

How to Make the Most of Your Offenses

*I myself always strive to have a conscience
without offense toward God and men.*

(ACTS 24:16)

Lately, I have seen a lot of strife and division in the church, which I'm convinced comes from Satan who stirs up offenses among Christians. I'm quite concerned about this and want to spend today and tomorrow sharing about this trap and how you can avoid it and deal with it.

You may think that, as Christians, we should never be offended or bothered with offenses, yet Jesus said offenses would come (see Matthew 18:7). But there's hope. Man has ways to deal with offenses, and God has ways to deal with offenses. I guarantee that with God's ways, you will fare better. In fact, the Lord showed me that offenses can be our best opportunities for miracles. I really believe that if the church today could learn how to handle offenses better, we'd live much better lives.

The word "offense" comes from the Greek word *skandalon*. It originally referred to the part of a trap to which the bait is attached, in other words, a snare. It's a hindrance that causes a fall. Therefore, an offense is a deliberately laid trap of the devil to get you or someone else to fall. He wants us so wrapped up in offenses that we never do what God has called us to do.

Look at David. David could easily have been offended and not killed Goliath at all. David went to the battle scene to bring food, but his older brother Eliab accused him otherwise: *"Why did you come down here?... I know your pride and the insolence of your heart, for you have come down to see the battle"* (1 Samuel 17:28). In other words, "You just came to see the fight!" David could have received it as an insult and chosen to be offended, but he didn't. Instead, he killed the giant. You will never kill your giants if you don't step over the offenses in your path.

Paul was stoned three times, whipped five times with 39 lashes each time, shipwrecked, and left for dead, yet he refused to be offended, saying, *"I myself always strive to have a conscience without offense toward God and men"* (Acts 24:16). Instead, Paul brought the good news to the gentiles, opened Europe to the gospel, and wrote the majority of the New Testament!

All kinds of offenses can beset us: we offend people, and people offend us; God offends us (ever get upset with God over an "unanswered" prayer?); and we get offended at ourselves. But you can be sure that inside every one of these offenses is a trap. You need to see just how tricky offenses are. Look and see how Satan is trying to throw you off course. Division, strife, stress, financial troubles, ill health, loneliness—these are the outcomes of falling into his traps. Holding on to an offense is a mental-attitude sin that reduces your faith. The Holy Spirit is hindered in your life, and you lose the anointing you want. But worse, you block what God can do for you. God says, *"I will return again to My place till they acknowledge their offense"* (Hosea 5:15).

God sees when people harbor any kind of offense, and He can't do anything until they acknowledge their offense. If you carry an offense, you will miss the miracle that God wants to make out of it. On the other hand, you can get great mileage for miracles out of offenses—like nothing else! You have to make a choice. Are you going to live offended (and be miserable), or are you going to forgive and get God's miracles?

Dealing with the Sting of Offenses

Who was delivered for our offenses, and was raised because of our justification.

(ROMANS 4:25)

When offenses come, and they will come, how can you recognize them as a trap from the devil and how can you deal with them?

First of all, let me tell you the wrong way to handle offenses. Don't run with your story to people who will say, "You poor little thing! How could they have done that to you?" Then the devil laughs and says, "Ha, ha, ha, I got a whole crowd in this time!" It's also just as important not to harbor an offense and become hard-hearted toward the offending person.

What you need to do is cast your burden of being offended on Jesus, *"Who was delivered for our offenses, and was raised because of our justification"* (Romans 4:25). You also need to pray and repent of your own offenses in the situation. If you try to prove that the other person is wrong and you are right, you can be sure that you are in the flesh and that your pride is in the way of what God wants to do.

Sometimes, after you pray and gain peace about the offense, the Lord will tell you to go to the other person to exhort him. Jesus gave us the steps (see Matthew 18:15–17). First, you go to the person who has offended you and try to reconcile with them. If that doesn't work, you're to take neutral, unbiased people with you to that person. If going to the person who offended you does not bring about reconciliation, then you're to go to the church. This doesn't mean everyone in the church, but rather the church leadership, people who are mature in the Lord.

But be careful! You have to be sure that the Lord wants you to go to the other person in the first place. If going to that person would only create more problems instead of "gaining you a brother or sister," just leave it with

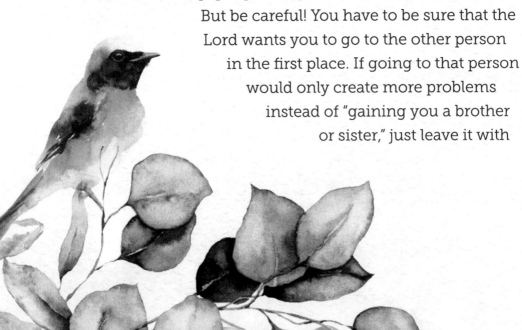

God. You don't need to carry offenses. Jesus came to carry them. Give them to Him, and He will give you miracles in return. Remember David. He constantly gave his offenses to the Lord, and David became a king!

One of the toughest things I have to do is stop people when they want me to listen to offenses as gossip instead of for reconciliation. Most people get offended when you have to say to them, even lovingly, "Hey, you need to go to the person involved and speak to him about it." Only the mature Christian will say, "You're right, and I appreciate your pointing out my mistake to me. I will go to the person directly involved."

Purpose in your heart right now to not be offended by anyone. Pray each morning in advance that you will forgive anyone who "trespasses against you." You will be amazed at how such a path of prayer will take the sting out of offenses and enable you to walk in love and truth. Stay in the Word. Psalm 119:165 (KJV) tells us, *"Great peace have they which love thy law: and nothing shall offend them."*

And remember, as a born-again Christian, you are in Christ. You have the same inherent temperament as Jesus, the man who was cursed, scorned, and crucified—yet who now reigns at the right hand of the Father. Like Jesus, we cannot afford the cost of holding on to offenses against ourselves or others.

Integrity & Faith

Integrity of the Heart

*The integrity of the upright will guide them, but
the perversity of the unfaithful will destroy them.*

(PROVERBS 11:3)

God wants you to be blessed in your health, relationships, finances, and in every area in which you have need. Sometimes we miss God's blessing because we try to cover up our shortcomings or hidden sins. But God will bless the person who openly confesses and forsakes the gray areas within their heart. The Bible calls that person full of "integrity," and that's the kind of person God wants you to be.

God wants us to be completely transparent with Him so that He can dispel any darkness we may try to hide. If there's some secret sin you're covering up, allow the Lord to cleanse your heart from any defilement so that you can begin to enjoy the benefits of integrity.

Integrity will guide you: *"The integrity of the upright will guide them, but the perversity of the unfaithful will destroy them"* (Proverbs 11:3). Sin in our lives will block God's directions for making right choices. Clear up any sin that may be hindering you from receiving God's instructions and godly wisdom. Integrity of the heart will make it easy for God to speak to you and make a straight path before you to follow.

Integrity will preserve and uphold you: *"Let integrity and uprightness preserve me, for I wait for You"* (Psalm 25:21). David knew that the benefits of integrity were long-lasting. In addition, your personal integrity will be evident to those around you, and it will be a protection in times of need. Look at Job. Even God commented on his integrity after he had lost everything he had, except a nagging wife (see Job 2:1–10).

He was so intent on maintaining his integrity that when he was defending his righteousness, he said, *"Let me be weighed on honest scales, that God may know my integrity"* (Job 31:6). In the end, God upheld him in his circumstances, and he was preserved.

Integrity will bless you. I believe that Christians don't have to be poor because God wants to meet all our needs according to His riches in glory (Philippians 4:19). And look at what Proverbs 19:1 says: *"Better is the poor who walks in his integrity than one who is perverse in his lips, and is a fool."* Do you see how important integrity is to God? God says it's better to have integrity and be poor than to have everything and be living in darkness.

It's okay to go to God with some dark spots in our hearts; He doesn't expect us to wait until our hearts are perfect before we approach Him. Let Him cleanse away the sin and darkness and set you free. Walking in integrity will allow God to bless you!

Your Anchor of Integrity

The righteous man walks in his integrity;
His children are blessed after him.

(PROVERBS 20:7)

When it seems like the world has gone crazy, anchor your-self to integrity, for it is a key to God's best. Even when you blow it, God can give you another chance and bring you through. God wants you to have integrity in every area, because integrity pays big dividends. Don't just go with the flow. Choose integrity and avoid the heart-wrenching consequences.

Integrity, or the lack of it, really shows up when you are under pressure. When the pressure is on, are you going to hold on to your anchor of integrity? Even if you've blown it and have not shown integrity at times, there's hope. Three of the Bible's greatest men—Abraham, Jacob, and Job—became men of integrity after acting just the opposite.

- Abraham "the Liar": Out of fear, Abraham lied two times, saying Sarah was his sister instead of his wife.
- Jacob "the Cheater": Jacob deceived his brother and his father. He manipulated his brother, Esau, into selling his birthright for a bowl of stew. Later, Jacob impersonated his brother to get all his father's blessings.
- Job "the Blamer": Job had an incredible number of trials. He became bitter with God and his friends and wished he had never been born. He felt like God had deserted him.

Under pressure, each of these men blew it. Yet each one made a quantum leap and developed integrity. God saw potential in these men of failed integrity, and He sees potential in you, too!

- God told Abraham to offer his son as a sacrifice (Genesis 22), and he obeyed. God called Abraham a "man of faith."
- Following his wrestling match with a man, God changed Jacob's name to "Israel" and even named the nation of Israel after him (Genesis 32:28).

- God Himself confronted Job and told him. "You are talking wrong, thinking wrong, and acting wrong. Look to me." Job repented, and God restored double everything he'd lost. (See Job 38–42.)

How did these men make such a quantum leap of change? They pursued God. The pursuit of godly integrity is well worth it.

- Integrity will preserve you: *"Keep my soul, and deliver me; let me not be ashamed, for I put my trust in You. Let integrity and uprightness preserve me, for I wait for You"* (Psalm 25:20–21).
- Integrity will uphold you: *"You uphold me in my integrity, and set me before Your face forever"* (Psalm 41:12).
- Integrity preserves your children: *"The righteous man walks in his integrity; his children are blessed after him"* (Proverbs 20:7).

If God could bring Abraham, Jacob, and Job through their messes, He will bring you through, too. Ask Jesus to help you learn integrity. Begin to study "integrity" in God's Word. Like Abraham, Jacob, and Job, integrity can be your anchor.

Walking in Integrity

*And Pharaoh said to his servants, "Can we find such
a one as this, a man in whom is the Spirit of God?"*
(GENESIS 41:38)

One of the key ingredients for living a successful, Christian life is integrity. Integrity is a character trait that should be at the foundation of our every thought and act. God wants integrity to so permeate the heart of a believer that every facet of their life reflects Jesus. The fruit of integrity is a life filled with success, as it was in Joseph's life: *The LORD made all he did to prosper in his hand"* (Genesis 39:3).

One time, a man in our church told me he was excited about a new business opportunity that would pay double his current salary—but it was in the pornography industry. He took the job, and eventually, his wife took the children and left him. In another instance, a woman I know became involved in adultery. It started when a man at her church complimented her on her appearance. When her husband was out of town, this man drove the woman and her children to church. The two spent more and more time together, and finally, they became involved immorally. Do you know what these people had in common? They both lacked integrity.

The Bible closely ties integrity in with the fear of the Lord. "Integrity" refers to "wholeness, completeness." Tied to the fear of the Lord, it implies "uprightness of character, state of being complete or undivided." Our new nature in Christ gives us the ability to live a life of integrity. A person of integrity is one whose soul and body acts like his born-again spirit. Only in God can we live a life of integrity. Any time we think we can do it on our own, we are going to fall. But when we look to God, He will help us do it. Integrity must come from our connection to God's heart. When we think of integrity, we often make the mistake of looking to ourselves to live the life of God. We can't, and we'll only blow it every time we try.

When we look to God to live His life of integrity through us, God will do it. Joseph was a man who walked with great integrity. Betrayed by his brothers, he refused to harbor bitterness in his heart. When Potiphar's wife tempted him, he fled from sin. In the midst of slavery and prison, Joseph feared God and kept his heart pure. Because he lived a life of integrity, Joseph exuded God and God's

victorious nature throughout his life: *"And Pharaoh said to his servants, 'Can we find such a one as this, a man in whom is the Spirit of God?'"* (Genesis 41:38).

The Word of God promises many benefits from walking in the fear of the Lord or in integrity:

- Wisdom: Proverbs 9:10
- Length of days: Proverbs 10:27
- Safety and refuge from the snare of the devil: Proverbs 14:26–27
- Riches, honor, and life: Proverbs 22:4
- Deliverance from evil: Proverbs 16:6

Walking in integrity brings many rewards. If you walk in the fear of the Lord, you can gain intimacy with God and be successful in your natural and spiritual life. Make integrity the goal, and God will work with you and through you to bring it to pass. He is faithful!

Walk by Faith

For we walk by faith, not by sight.
(2 CORINTHIANS 5:7)

The Christians who are affecting and transforming lives in a dramatic way are those who know that faith is the secret to everything they do. Look at the courageous Christians in China and the Middle East. They *"walk by faith, not by sight"* (2 Corinthians 5:7). The threat of persecution is ever-present. In order to survive and spread the gospel, they must live daily on a greater level of faith than many of us in freer countries can imagine. We may not face the same dangers they do, but does that mean we can relax in our faith? No! We need to have faith for miracles right where we are.

You may say, "Faith is important, but it's not the most important." I'm not knocking things other than faith; but you have to have faith before you can have anything else. Romans 1:17 says, *"For in it the righteousness of God is revealed from*

faith to faith; as it is written, 'The just shall live by faith.'" You were saved by grace—through faith (Ephesians 2:8)—and now God wants you to live by faith. If that's how you're supposed to live, then faith must be important! It is important to keep your faith active if you plan to be an effective, productive Christian.

Faith is different because it is not in your sensory realm. Faith takes you into the supernatural realm so that you can have God's supernatural miracles. In other words, faith brings God's substance from heaven into your earthly life.

Christians in communist and Islamic countries are overcoming much evil through their faith. Because of that, they are successful soul winners who see many miracles. *"For whatever is born of God overcomes the world. And this is the victory that has overcome the world—our faith"* (1 John 5:4). You don't

have to be in the midst of a trial to use your faith. You may just have some goals and dreams for which you are aiming. Those are hopes, and Hebrews 11:1 says that it takes faith to see those hopes fulfilled: *"Now faith is the substance of things hoped for, the evidence of things not seen."*

The key to receiving your substance of faith is through God's Word, which tells you what God has for you. If I had never read, *"The seed of the righteous shall be delivered"* (Proverbs 11:21 KJV), I would never have known that God had deliverance planned for my children. If your faith is going to reach into heaven to get substance for your life, then you'd better know what's available.

Set your goals by finding the promises in God's Word and by using your faith for those things. Do you want to do great things? Do you want to accomplish your goals and see the victories God has for you? Then bone up on faith! Romans 10:17 tells you that faith comes by hearing God's Word. You need to hear about faith every chance you get. Don't just read this and walk away from it. Read it with the intention of receiving a rejuvenation of faith in your spirit so that you can overcome whatever trial you are experiencing right now!

Need a "Faith Lift"?

*And the Lord said to Abram, after Lot had
separated from him: "Lift your eyes now and
look from the place where you are..."*

(GENESIS 13:14)

There was a time in my life when I thought, *God, where are you?* To be honest, I guess I was disappointed with God. Although I prayed and prayed, spoke the Word, and did all I knew how to do, it seemed that the answer I wanted just wasn't coming fast enough. That disappointment with God led to depression. I didn't want to feel that way, but I didn't know what to do about it either.

One day, the Lord said to me, "Marilyn, you're not the first person to experience depression. In fact, some of the greatest

people of faith in the Bible went through the same emotions, but they came out of it when they looked away from their circumstance and looked to me instead."

Today I want to help you get the upward look that can change any depression you might be feeling into a sense of God's love, care, and provision for your deepest desires. You don't have to be down and out; you can be up and over, even in the midst of the most depressing situation.

Abraham, the father of faith, had plenty of opportunities to feel depressed. God had called him into the promised land, and when he got there, he was met with a famine. Abraham's herdsmen fought with Lot's herdsmen, and finally, the contention was so great that the two families split up—leaving Abraham to live in the dry, desolate mountain area.

Abraham could have said, "God, you told me to come to the promised land, but there's not much promise here! And now Lot has taken the best grazing land and left me with nothing but sand and rocks." But notice God's answer to Abraham's depression: *"And the Lord said to Abram, after Lot had separated from him: 'Lift your eyes now and look from the place where you are—northward, southward, eastward, and westward'"* (Genesis 13:14).

"Look up, Abraham," the Lord was saying. "Don't look at what you *don't* have or even at what you *do* have. Look instead at what I am going to do for you." And what was God going to do for Abraham? God was going to give him all the land that he could see in every direction!

But Abraham's greatest challenge was yet to come. God told him to sacrifice Isaac, his only child! Abraham had the opportunity to be depressed, but he was obedient, and they set out for Mount Moriah, where he *"lifted his eyes"* (Genesis 22:4), and Isaac's life was spared. I think that was when he began to get a faith vision of the miracle God was going to do. We need to get the same upward look that sees the miracles God has for us.

What about your situation? Is there a promise that you've claimed from God's Word that you are waiting to see fulfilled? Don't look at what you don't have—keep the upward look by focusing on what God has promised. There's no room for depression when you're seeing only God's provision for your need! Remember, God can change your worst situation if you'll just look up!

The Faith Fight

Without faith it is impossible to please Him, for He
who comes to God must believe that He is, and that
He is a rewarder of those who diligently seek Him.

(HEBREWS 11:6)

A key to faith is found in 1 Timothy 6:12: *"Fight the good fight of faith."* Were you ever in a fight? Did you win? If so, how? Is faith going to involve a fight? Yes, but the way you fight is your key to victory.

Have you ever fought the devil? Forget it! You can't beat the tiniest demon in hell. Even if you blindfolded him, tied his arms behind his back, and stopped up his ears—he'd still win. Why? Because flesh and blood cannot fight spiritual battles. The only fight you can win is the fight of faith because Jesus already defeated the devil for you. Your battle isn't against the devil. It's a battle to keep holding on to and believing God's Word. Don't fight the devil; just let him know that he's already been defeated by Jesus.

When the devil comes against us, we want to say, "He's trying to get my money," or "He's after my health and my peace." "He's after my kids." But that's not really true. The devil is after your faith. If he can separate you from faith, then he can convince you that you've lost the fight, and you will be defeated. Don't ever be complacent about the power of faith, because only by faith will you win over the devil's attacks and glorify God.

Once I heard someone say, "The devil is afraid of Christians." I asked God, "If he is afraid of Christians, why is he walking all over so many of them?" The Lord showed me, "The devil is only afraid of Christians with faith." Your faith is your victory!

Do you want to please God? Hebrews 11:6 tells you that, *"Without faith it is impossible to please Him."* Every time you get your faith out and believe for something you are hoping for, do you please God? Yes!

How do you start faith that pleases God? Hebrews 11:6 continues, *"He who comes to God must believe that He* [God] *is."* Believe that

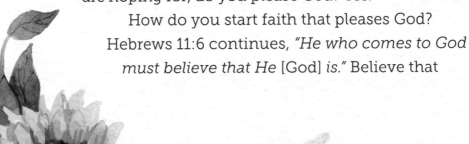

God is there listening and watching when you pray. You can't just pray and then an hour later say, "God probably didn't hear me." That's why it's important to remember that the last part of Hebrews 11:6 says, *"He is a rewarder of those who diligently seek Him."*

If you're thinking, "I haven't been diligent in faith," then renew your faith covenant with God. Maybe you have heard about faith without really applying it to your life. Think of your biggest hopes and then decide to have faith for them. People in the world say, "I wouldn't get my hopes up." But Christians should get their hopes up and then stand in faith believing for the hoped-for results.

God wants you to be full of hope and living by faith so that you are a witness to the world as you walk in victory. With a faith walk, you can cross the border from a life of mediocrity to one of miracles!

Faith Answers

"Get out of your country, from your family and from
your father's house, to a land that I will show you.
I will make you a great nation; I will bless you and
make your name great; and you shall be a blessing."

(GENESIS 12:1–2)

Many people ask me why it seems like some Christians have an easier time obeying God than others. The answer is that these people have a vision from God inside them, and those visions produce the faith they need to do what God wants them to do! When you catch hold of God's vision, the word "quit" is erased from your vocabulary, and you can say, "My dreams will come true because God gave them to me, and I believe they will come to pass."

It had to be hard for Noah to spend years upon years trying to explain what he was doing to a world full of people who had never even seen rain, let alone a flood. I picture people taking their families out by Noah's ark for after-dinner strolls just to laugh at him before they went to bed.

He may have lost friends and family, yet even with decades of persecution, Noah continued to build, believe, preach, and pray. He could have become depressed, discouraged, and given up; but he kept at it because he had caught ahold of God's vision, and His vision gave him faith that survived and surpassed the trials he faced.

I've learned over the years that even the smallest portion of a vision will produce faith. This is important because God sometimes doesn't give you the entire vision at once. Consider Abraham. When God called him out of his father's house and his native land, He didn't tell him the vision He had for him. God simply said, "Go." Only when Abraham arrived at his destination did God show him His vision of being the father of a multitude, the father of a nation (see Genesis 12–13).

The vision was so important to *Abram's* life that God changed his name, which means "father of altitudes," to *Abraham*, which means "father of multitudes." (Imagine having God change your name to reinforce the power of His vision for your life!) However, even after Abraham's faith was greatly energized by

his encounter with God, he started to second-guess God when nothing happened for 11 years. He finally went along with Sarah's plan for him to have a baby with her servant Hagar.

There may be times in your life when your vision seems to die. I'm sure that by the time Abraham and Sarah entered their 90s and still didn't have a baby, they thought, *God, it's physically impossible for us to bear a child. It's too late.* Did they begin to wonder if the vision came from God after all? Abraham and Sarah's vision of a family still had not come to pass. But when it was too late for *them* to have a baby, God took over, created life supernaturally, and Isaac was born.

He may do the same with you. If you tend to give yourself the glory when good things happen, God may keep your dreams out of reach. Then, when you finally admit you can't do it, God delivers your miracle.

Do you have an "Isaac" waiting to be birthed in your life? It's not too late. Don't give up! Allow God to take over to deliver your miracle.

A Mother's Faith

The seed of the righteous shall be delivered.

(PROVERBS 11:21 KJV)

Whether they are grown and living a life of sin or still peacefully at home under your influence, the transforming power of God's Word is available to help your children. God promises that *"The seed of the righteous shall be delivered"* (Proverbs 11:21 KJV).

There is something unique about a mother's faith. Remember how the Syrophoenician mother reached out in supernatural faith on behalf of her hurting daughter? She begged Jesus to heal her demon-possessed daughter, but Jesus ignored her. She persisted, and finally, Jesus said:

> *"I was not sent except to the lost sheep of the house of Israel."*
>
> *Then she came and worshiped Him, saying, "Lord, help me!"*

*But He answered and said, "It is not good to take
the children's bread and throw it to the little dogs."*

*And she said, "Yes, Lord, yet even the little dogs eat
the crumbs which fall from their masters' table."*

*Then Jesus answered and said to her,
"O woman, great is your faith! Let it be to you
as you desire." And her daughter was healed
from that very hour.* (MATTHEW 15:24–28)

This woman was not about to let anything stop her from claiming God's transforming power for her daughter. Your children need that same kind of spiritual tenacity exerted on their behalf. Put your faith in God and His Word. Although your children may be involved in ungodly lifestyles, don't let go of God's transforming power. Remember the Prodigal Son. The Bible says, *"he came to himself"* (Luke 15:17). In other words, his eyes were suddenly opened, and he saw things from the perspective

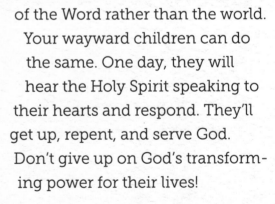

of the Word rather than the world. Your wayward children can do the same. One day, they will hear the Holy Spirit speaking to their hearts and respond. They'll get up, repent, and serve God. Don't give up on God's transforming power for their lives!

You hold the key. Your faith in God's power to transform can determine the course of your child's life. Look at Moses's mother, Jochebed. Pharaoh ordered all the newborn male Hebrews to be murdered, but Jochebed trusted in God, *"So the woman conceived and bore a son. . . . she hid him three months"* (Exodus 2:2). Jochebed had a mother's faith for her baby. She hid him, then put him in an ark and floated him down a river full of crocodiles. The baby ended up in the bathtub of Pharaoh's daughter. She named him "Moses" and raised him as her own. Because of his mother's faith, Moses's life was spared. He received an education and had the best of everything. It wasn't until after committing murder and running away that Moses answered the call of God and was used of the Lord in tremendous ways. Looking back on the circumstances of Moses's birth, no one would have foreseen all of this in his future. God's transforming power turned Moses's life around.

Maybe your decisions haven't always served God, and you've made some mistakes in raising your children. The good news is, regardless of their beginnings, God has plans for your children—they may be future deliverers in the body of Christ. Stop feeling guilty about past mistakes! Seek God and repent. Stand on His Word—the transforming power for their lives—and see what God does.

Prayer

Supercharged Prayer

Pray without ceasing.

(1 THESSALONIANS 5:17)

Christians who have accepted Jesus Christ as Lord and Savior can have a relationship with the Father. Jesus said, *"I am the way, the truth, and the life. No one comes to the Father except through Me"* (John 14:6). And prayer is the communication method you must use to develop that relationship. If you want a supercharged prayer life, keep reading!

Follow God's directions for prayer, and you will get the results you desire. Jesus told us to pray to the Father in His name. When you do, two-thirds of the Trinity pray with you—Jesus and the Holy Spirit. Romans 8:27 says that the Holy Spirit intercedes for us according to the will of God. Hebrews 7:25 says that Jesus ever lives to intercede for us. We don't pray *to* Jesus or *to* the Holy Spirit. They pray for us according to the Father's will. Also, John 16:23 indicates that your prayers are established when you pray to the Father because you have two extremely powerful intercessors agreeing with you. How can you lose?

Paul tells us in 1 Thessalonians 5:17 to *"pray without ceasing."* It doesn't mean we quit working and stay home praying all day. God gave us the gift of praying in the Spirit so that we could communicate with Him any time. So, whatever you're doing or wherever you are, find opportunities to pray and communicate with God.

If you are believing for something you haven't received, check your heart. Second Timothy 2:22 tells us to call upon the Lord with a pure heart. Examine your heart and be sensitive to God's leading. If you have unconfessed sin, repent. Then your slate will be clean, and you can expect an answer to your prayer. Ask God if you're doing something wrong, and look out! You'll get the swiftest answer! When David asked God what they were doing wrong to have experienced a three-year drought, God answered, David acted on it, and the drought ended. (See 2 Samuel 21:1–14.)

Your prayer life will also be affected if you lose sight of others' needs. Proverbs 21:13 says, *"Whoever shuts his ears to the cry of the poor will also cry himself and not be heard."* Spend at least one hour a week praying for someone else. If you show compassion for others' lives, you will see powerful changes in your own life. Remember, you reap what you sow.

Finally, to see answers to prayer, you must release your faith in God's ability. The woman with the issue of blood knew exactly what she wanted from the Lord—healing. She released her faith and was instantly healed (Mark 5:27–28). Act on your faith!

No matter what is happening in your life now, seek out your heavenly Father in prayer as often as you can. Remember to pray to the Father in Jesus's name and pray in the Spirit without ceasing. Examine your heart, repent if necessary, and you'll free God's hands to answer your prayers. Show compassion to others, and don't forget to release your faith. Prayer is quick, efficient, and available to you right now!

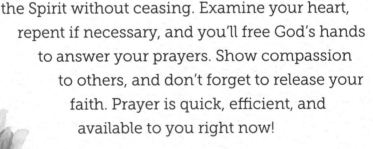

P.U.S.H.

*Then another angel, having a golden censer, came
and stood at the altar. He was given much incense,
that he should offer it with the prayers of all the saints
upon the golden altar which was before the throne.
And the smoke of the incense, with the prayers of the
saints, ascended before God from the angel's hand.*

(REVELATION 8:3–4)

If I told you I have the answer to every problem in your life,
wouldn't you like to know what it is? Well, it's prayer! That's
because, without a good prayer life, we are powerless.

If you are praying and not getting answers, examine your
prayer life. If you just drop in on God once a week, it's not going
to work. Only effective, fervent prayer will change things (see
James 5:16). Elijah's prayers brought the widow's son back to
life (1 Kings 17:23), proclaimed a drought (1 Kings 17:1), and then
three years later, called an end to the drought (1 Kings 18:41).

Prayer will give you purpose. When you pray, your heart
touches God's heart, and you begin to pray God's purpose. God
looks for somebody who will get in unity with Him. It's easy for
us to tell Him everything that's wrong with our government,

church, or family. God's not looking for gap finders—He has plenty of them! He's looking for gap-standers: people who will stand in the gap with Him and pray His will. Moses's compassion for the people prompted him to stand in the gap for the Israelites when God threatened to wipe them out. In fact, he said, "God, if you blot them out, then blot me out, too." He prayed, and God spared them.

Our prayers are precious to God. Look at Revelation 8:3–4:

> *Then another angel, having a golden censer,*
> *came and stood at the altar. He was given*
> *much incense, that he should offer it with the*
> *prayers of all the saints upon the golden altar*
> *which was before the throne. And the smoke*
> *of the incense, with the prayers of the saints,*
> *ascended before God from the angel's hand.*

Prayers rise with the incense on the golden altar before the throne of God! When we pray, it is sweet, smells good, and it goes up! Our prayers activate God's angels, and they move because we pray God's Word. God thinks our prayers are so important. He puts them on a golden altar and says, "Mmm, they smell good."

When you pray God's purpose, you will pray His provision to meet the need. This is intercession, and intercession means "to come between." We can all intercede—we can pray and change things. There are great examples of intercession in

Nehemiah 2–4. Nehemiah saved Jerusalem with his prayers. Abigail interceded for her cruel husband and saved his life (1 Samuel 25). Conversely, Isaiah 59:16 says that God looked and looked but found not one person to intercede. God is looking for people who will stand in the gap. What about you? Can you stand in the gap for others so that God doesn't have to look any further?

One last secret to an effective prayer life is P.U.S.H.—pray until something happens! Don't give up! God doesn't always work in our timing. Sometimes it may seem He's never going to answer. That's when the devil wants you to give up. That's when you have to P.U.S.H.! What's going to rescue you or your family? Pay your overdue bills? Heal you or your loved one? Your stubborn prayers! Prayer that never ceases changes things. So P.U.S.H.!

Hide and Seek

*Give ear to my prayer, O God, and do not
hide Yourself from my supplication.*

(PSALM 55:1)

*I*t can be discouraging when you pray for something for a long time, and it doesn't come to pass. It can seem that God is hiding from you. David felt the same way. In Psalm 55:1, David cried out, *"Give ear to my prayer, O God, and do not hide Yourself from my supplication."* Do you feel like God is hiding from your prayer? And, what do you do when it seems like God is hiding?

When God seems to hide, persist! *"Ask, and it will be given to you; seek, and you will find; knock, and it will be opened to you. For everyone who asks receives, and he who seeks finds, and to him who knocks it will be opened"* (Matthew 7:7–8). The words "ask," "seek," and "knock" are in a Greek verb tense that indicates

continuous action—prayer must be ongoing. We must persist in asking, persevere in seeking, and continue knocking until we prevail. Do not stop praying! If you allow yourself to become discouraged and give up, you can miss your answer. If you have already given up praying for something or someone—repent and start praying again.

According to James 5:16, *"The effective, fervent prayer of a righteous man avails much."* The word "effective" in Greek means "energy." Your prayers have energy! When you pray fervently, you release the energy of God into a situation.

When God seems to hide, change! There are times when God delays answering prayer because He is changing you. You may not be able to handle the answer to your prayer until you are different. When you pray for a situation, particularly for something that has to do with you, God will deal with you first. Sometimes God isn't hiding from your prayer; He's actually trying to get your attention about something in your life that He wants to change. Often, that change is a process, and it may take time. We sometimes think God is slow to answer, but what if He is waiting on us?

Consider Joseph. As a 17-year-old, God gave Joseph dreams that one day his entire family would bow before him. All the trials and tribulations he endured over the next 13 years prepared Joseph to step into his miracle. At the age of 30, Joseph became prime minister of the mightiest, most advanced nation on earth, Egypt. It was well worth the delay and the changes Joseph had to make to receive his blessings, and it will be worth it for you, too!

When God seems to hide, expand your faith! It is through *"faith and patience* [we] *inherit the promises"* (Hebrews 6:12). Nothing comes from God except by faith and patience. Abraham, whom we call the "Father of Faith," waited 25 years for his promised son to be born. He made some serious mistakes during those years. At times he lied. He even tried to "help" God fulfill His promise, and the results were disastrous. Despite his mistakes, he developed great faith, even to the point that he believed that God could raise his son from the dead if he sacrificed him. God will delay answers to prayer to build your faith, too.

These are the end times. God needs people who are persistent, conformed to His image, and powerful in faith. When God seems to hide, you need to persist until you prevail! Become like Elijah, who prayed seven times before it rained. Moses prayed 40 days for people who were murmuring. Daniel prayed for three weeks before he heard from God. Jesus prayed all night before he chose His disciples. Each of these people persisted until God answered their prayer. So, when it seems as if God is hiding, don't give up! Pray until you win!

Becoming International Influencers

"Ask of Me, and I will give You the nations for Your inheritance, and the ends of the earth for Your possession." **(PSALM 2:8)**

You may never visit another country or serve as a missionary, yet God wants to use you to influence nations. As a Christian, you have responsibilities to the nations of the world. The Bible shows that from the beginning of creation, God has been concerned about nations, and you should be, too.

There is no reference to nations or countries until after the flood (see Genesis 10:25–32). God used individuals to build nations and determine their boundaries (see Deuteronomy 32:8). Each of Noah's sons became fathers of nations. Shem's descendants were the line from which the Jewish and Arab nations were born. Japheth's descendants nationalized the Indo-European countries. Ham's descendants formed the African nations. Shem's son Eber then had two sons:

The name of one was Peleg; for in his days the earth was divided; and his brother's name was Joktan.... These were the families of the sons of Noah, according to their generations, in their nations; and from these the nations were divided on the earth after the flood. (GENESIS 10:25, 32)

God wanted a nation of His own. God's original plan was to start with just one man, then that man's descendants would become a nation of priests and take the Word of God to the world. He chose the seed of Abraham to be that nation. But the Israelites failed over and over again. Fortunately, Moses interceded for Israel, and God spared them. When the Israelites entered Canaan, they were to be a nation set apart to God, unlike the ungodly, sinful Canaanites. However, the Israelites became like the Canaanites, worshiping false gods and serving idols rather than the one true God. They now needed a priest themselves; God chose the tribe of Levi to be priests for the Jewish nation and to keep them in line. When they failed, God started over again with another individual, one who was perfect in every way and would not fail—Jesus.

God did something very special that affected you and me. Everyone who has professed belief in Jesus has become a citizen of the nation of God. First Peter 2:9 says, *"But you are a chosen generation, a* royal priesthood, a holy nation, His own special people, that you may proclaim the praises of Him who called you out of darkness into His marvelous light." That means we are God's nation of priests—royal priests at that—and have been entrusted with His plan to bring God's light to the nations. We have become the nation of priests that God always wanted.

The citizens of God's nation are scattered around the world, and His kingdom knows no boundaries. God has priests in every corner of the world. Even when countries attempt to blot out Christianity, God knows how to get His priests into those countries. You don't actually have to travel to another country to affect it. You can stay home and have an impact on other nations by prayer. Your prayers can topple ungodly, oppressive governments. Your prayers can open the doors of countries that are locked up tight. Prayer is your passport to the world.

Our priesthood is royal and limitless. As a royal priest of the King of Kings, you have authority over worldly kings: *"Ask of Me, and I will give You the nations for Your inheritance, and the ends of the earth for Your possession"* (Psalm 2:8). Through prayer and intercession, you can bind the ungodly actions of an earthly king and loose what God wants to do in a nation. We don't need visas and passports to bring nations to their knees. We need righteousness because *"Righteousness exalts a nation"* (Proverbs 14:34). And we need the *"effective, fervent prayer of a righteous man"* (James 5:16). Those are our prayers—yours and mine!

Pray to Change the World

*"Those who are wise shall shine like the brightness
of the firmament, and those who turn many to
righteousness like the stars forever and ever."*

(DANIEL 12:3)

D o you want to shine as the brightness of the firmament, full of God's glory? You will reap vast, eternal riches when you pray for nations. Perhaps you cannot personally go and minister God's Word in the uttermost parts of the earth, but your prayers will touch the people who are there; and they can touch the people who bring the gospel into those countries.

God is even preparing the hearts of the people for whom He wants you to pray. Therefore, it is important for you to esteem His priorities and to pray for nations:

*Therefore I exhort first of all that supplications,
prayers, intercessions, and giving of thanks be
made for all men, for kings and all who are in
authority, that we may lead a quiet and peaceable
life in all godliness and reverence.* **(1 TIMOTHY 2:1–2)**

You may ask, "How do I do that?" You can obey this Scripture by praying each day for a nation and for that nation's leader. Here are some guidelines that God has given us for effective prayer.

1. Pray that decisions against the gospel will be brought to confusion. Psalm 109:29 says, *"Let my accusers . . . cover themselves with their own disgrace as with a mantle."* We must put the devil's work to confusion because a house divided against itself cannot stand.

2. Pray that leaders who live in spiritual darkness will receive a personal message of God's love and repent of their evil ways. Second Chronicles 33 tells about Manasseh, who was so evil that history says he had the prophet Isaiah sawed in half. After 55 years of wickedness, the Assyrians took Manasseh and his nation into captivity.

While in prison, Manasseh sought God and repented of his evil. God restored Manasseh to the throne, and he led the entire nation to repentance! Likewise, we should never look at any ruler and say, "He will never change."

3. Pray that leaders will find knowledge and wisdom in God's Word. I pray this Scripture for our president every day: *"The king's heart is in the hand of the LORD, like the rivers of water; He turns it wherever He wishes"* (Proverbs 21:1). When you claim this verse for those in authority, you are loosing the power of God's divine direction on their behalf.

4. Pray that leaders in war-torn nations will grow
    weary of bloodshed. I believe that spirits of violence
    cause leaders to become power-hungry. Bind these
    powers, principalities, and rulers of darkness in
    the name of Jesus; exalt the name of Jesus over
    those nations (Ephesians 6:12). Pray that war-torn
    countries will find rest and peace in Jesus!

5. Pray that leaders will know that their earthly
    kingdoms were given by God. Nebuchadnezzar ruled
    the greatest empire that the world had ever known
    (see Daniel 2). One day, he exalted himself and said,
    "Look at this great kingdom that I built!" Even history
    acknowledges that the man went stark-raving mad.
    Seven years later, he looked up to heaven, began
    praising the Lord, and his sanity returned! Fervently
    pray that rulers will praise God—not themselves!

By faith, you can decree salvation unto the uttermost parts of
the earth (see Hebrews 11:33). Decree the salvation of nations by
faith—your faith pleases the Lord. Dedicate yourself to pray for
the nations in the uttermost parts of the earth. Your intercession
can turn nations to eternal righteousness, and you will shine as
the stars forever and ever!

Challenges

Avoiding the Perils of Anger

Cease from anger, and forsake wrath;
do not fret—it only causes harm.

(PSALM 37:8)

Anger, more than any other thing, is responsible for getting people into trouble, destroying lives, and ending relationships. It can cause us to miss God's blessing, short-circuit our anointing, and hurt the very people we are called to bless.

We all have gotten angry and blown it; yet, it doesn't have to be that way. Anger, if released inappropriately, will devour your blessing. God says very clearly in Psalm 37:8: *"Cease from anger, and forsake wrath; do not fret—it only causes harm."*

Everyone recognizes feelings of anger, yet many people aren't aware of a deceptive form of anger that I call "camouflaged anger." Camouflaged anger is murmuring, criticizing, complaining, and quarreling.

For 40 years, the Israelites grumbled and complained their way through the wilderness. They murmured about Moses, the food, and the occasional lack of water; they even complained because they didn't have leeks and onions! Their murmuring cost them the promised land, and murmuring could cost you the same. First Corinthians 10:9–10 says: "*Nor let us tempt Christ, as some of them also tempted, and were destroyed by serpents; nor complain, as some of them also complained, and were destroyed by the destroyer.*"

Whining, murmuring, criticizing, and complaining are evidence of a "victim mentality." If you have been abused or mistreated, the worst thing you can do is to continually think of yourself as a victim. A victim mentality will tie you to painful memories your whole life.

The good news is that there is a way to break free! Follow these simple steps:

1. Delay venting or taking action while you are angry: *"A fool vents all his feelings, but a wise man holds them back"* (Proverbs 29:11).

2. Ask the Holy Spirit to guide you: *"When He, the Spirit of truth, has come, He will guide you into all truth..."* (John 16:13).

3. Pray for people who hurt you: *"Love your enemies, bless those who curse you, do good to those who hate you, and pray for those who spitefully use you and persecute you"* (Matthew 5:44).

The cost of anger is far too great. Its fee is in the things you hold most dear—lost relationships, abandoned blessings, blocked anointing, and even your health. Decide now to deal with your anger. Ask God to help you bring it under control, empower you to forgive, and heal the wounds others have inflicted. Only when God helps you to manage anger will you be able to come into your personal promised land of peace, provision, and victory.

Who's the Boss?

"Behold, I give you the authority to trample on serpents and scorpions, and over all the power of the enemy, and nothing shall by any means hurt you."

(LUKE 10:19)

When Wally and I first started pastoring, we called on every family who came to our church. Some homes we visited were warm and loving; others seemed cold, empty, broken, and without love. Maybe you feel your house is cold, empty, or broken. There may be things left over from your family's past, such as generational curses of alcohol, drugs, strife, confusion, divorce, pornography, violence, or anger. I have good news for you—it doesn't have to stay that way.

Jesus has given you authority over the enemy and all his evil schemes, *"Behold, I give you the authority to trample on serpents and scorpions, and over all the power of the enemy, and nothing shall by any means hurt you"* (Luke 10:19). If you want peace in your home, using that God-given authority, you must first evict the "strong man." Matthew 12:29 says, *"How can one enter a strong man's house and plunder his goods, unless he first binds the strong man? And then he will plunder his house."*

The only way you can plunder the strong man and reclaim your home is through Jesus. You can have good intentions for the welfare of your family, but if Jesus isn't Lord, you will have a problem. If Jesus isn't at the helm of your ship, one stronger than you will steer your life on a course for the jagged rocks of destruction.

Making Jesus Lord is only the beginning. He must stay Lord. Jesus warned us, saying:

> *"When an unclean spirit goes out of a man, he goes through dry places, seeking rest, and finds none. Then he says, 'I will return to my house from which I came.' And when he comes, ... he goes and takes with him seven other spirits more wicked than himself, ... and the last state of that man is worse than the first."* **(MATTHEW 12:43–45)**

When your house is cleansed, and Jesus is made Lord, demons that have lived there for generations flee, but they will attempt to regain entry. If the demon succeeds this time, it will come back with seven spirits that are worse. It's important to not only make Jesus Lord of your house and family but to make sure He *remains* master. Use the authority Jesus gave you when the devil comes marching up to your door—then bind him and kick him out!

Years ago, a young man called me desperately seeking help. His wife kept threatening to leave him. I advised him to take authority in their home. When he began praying and reading his Bible daily, something began to happen. His wife became as spiritually turned on as he was. Eventually, they even became assistant pastors! The turnaround started when he made Jesus master and believed He could take them through their challenging situation.

Prayer is the foundation for everything. Establish Jesus's authority in your household through prayer. As a Spirit-filled Christian, you have the Holy Spirit to strengthen you as you pray and stand against the enemy of your family and home. Ask, believe, and take your God-given place of authority over your house. Make Jesus the master of your home, and He will turn the situation around. With the living Word at the head of your home, the devil and his ways will never again have a foothold.

Hard-to-Love People

"Then the children of Judah and the children of Israel shall be gathered together, and appoint for themselves one head; and they shall come up out of the land, for great will be the day of Jezreel!"

(HOSEA 1:11)

Our family relationships can serve as mirrors of our spiritual lives, just like Hosea's family was a symbol of Israel's treatment of God. This story has implications for us, for we see the heart of God and His grace and compassion for us when we blow it. It also teaches us to have compassion and grace for others when they blow it. God wants us to be *receivers* of grace and *givers*, too. That's why the story of Hosea is so important to understand. It's a graphic portrayal of God's reaction when His children go astray through sin and seek the world instead of Him.

In the book of Hosea, the Israelites had gotten so far into idolatry that God regularly sent prophets to warn them of their pending captivity, yet they continued in their adulterous ways. So, God spoke to the prophet Hosea and told him to marry Gomer, a prostitute (Hosea 1:2–3). Hosea obeyed the Lord, married Gomer, and their son, Jezreel, was born. Each child born of Gomer would carry a prophetic name, and Jezreel was no exception. Jezreel means, "God sows," which not only indicated that he was Hosea's son but that God would be merciful to Israel in the future.

The Jezreel Valley was the site of many battles in the Old Testament—and it is also the future site of the battle of Armageddon. By telling Hosea to name his son Jezreel, God was saying that He would turn the tide of the Jewish nation at the end of the age in the Jezreel Valley. God would reverse the trend toward destruction, and Jezreel would become a place of hope for the people, for He would once again call His people back to Himself: *"Then the children of Judah and the children of Israel shall be gathered together, and appoint for themselves one head; and they shall come up out of the land, for great will be the day of Jezreel!"* (Hosea 1:11).

When Gomer's daughter was born, God told Hosea to: *"Call her name Lo-Ruhamah, for I will no longer have mercy on the house of Israel, but I will utterly take them away'"* (Hosea 1:6). In Hebrew, "Lo" means "no." "Lo" in front of a word means "no" or "not," so her name means "no mercy." Also, this child was not

Hosea's. The symbolism here is that the nation of Israel is not God's, and He will no longer have mercy on it. Unfortunately, things would get worse before they got better. This deteriorating relationship between God and Israel is pictured in the birth of Gomer's next child: *"She conceived and bore a son. Then God said: 'Call his name Lo-Ammi, for you are not My people, and I will not be your God'"* (Hosea 1:8–9). *Lo-Ammi* means "not my people." God is saying that Israel is no more His people than Lo-Ammi is Hosea's child. Were this marriage not ordained by God, this is the place where Hosea could have said, "Forget it! This woman is playing the harlot." But by sticking it out, Hosea is showing us something about God's compassion and grace.

Hosea's marriage to Gomer is like God's marriage to Israel, and it's symbolic of the Christian's covenant relationship with God. There are a lot of things that can lure you away from reading the Word or from prayer. It hurts Him because we are His bride, just like it hurt Hosea to know that his wife was unfaithful to him. However, God continues to love us and extend His compassion and grace to us. Be true to Him, and don't stray!

The Grace Escape

"And I will have mercy on her who had not obtained mercy; then I will say to those who were not My people, 'You are My people!' And they shall say, 'You are my God!'"

(HOSEA 2:23)

We are adopted into the family of God, much like Hosea apparently adopted Lo-Ruhamah and Lo-Ammi. Hosea doesn't use the "Lo" in front of the children's names when he asks them to go tell their mother to return to him (Hosea 2:1–2). He is raising them as his own. He's saying,"You are mine. I will have mercy." He's a blessing to them. Likewise, God blesses us even when we act like thugs! You see, one believing mate sanctifies the household. If you will stand for your house, your sanctification, faith, grace, and wisdom will sanctify your household (see 1 Corinthians 7:14).

Despite her behavior, Hosea is still willing to provide for Gomer's needs. She left him, thinking her needs were being met by her lovers, but we learn that it was Hosea who gave her grain, wine, oil, silver, and gold (see Hosea 2:8). She depended on the world, thinking the more men she slept with, the more money she'd have. Her priorities were in the wrong place.

Sometimes when your priorities are wrong, God will let you go into the wilderness: *"Therefore, behold, I will allure her, will bring her into the wilderness, and speak comfort to her"* (Hosea 2:14). There He will speak comfort to you, wooing you all over again. In so doing, He makes the place of your judgment into a place of hope. The place of your sin and failure can become the place of your biggest hope because God is a God of grace. As the God of grace, He says, *"I will have mercy on her who had not obtained mercy; then I will say to those who were not My people, 'You are My people!' And they shall say, 'You are my God!'"* (Hosea 2:23).

This grace truly comes into play when Hosea goes to buy Gomer off the slave block. By this point, Gomer has become repulsive to her lovers, and no one wants her—except Hosea. God told him to love her again, just as He loves Israel, which left Him and committed spiritual adultery. Eventually, God told him she would call him *"Ishi"* instead of "Baali." *Ishi* means "my husband," and *Baali* means "my lord." Once he bought her, it meant he owned her. If she were to leave him again, then it would be legal for him to have her killed. But Hosea is saying he will be her husband, not her master, and love her (see Hosea 2:16).

How could Gomer resist a love like that? The Bible tells us she went back to him and never left him again. Likewise, Israel would eventually be restored and remain true to God: *"I will heal their backsliding, I will love them freely, for My anger has turned away from him"* (Hosea 14:4). When Israel was taken captive into Assyria, they realized what they had lost. After their captivity, they never again went after strange gods and remained true to God. So, if He can heal Gomer and a nation, doesn't that mean He can also heal us and our nation of backsliding? Yes! Absolutely, yes!

Keys to a Successful Marriage

*The secret of the LORD is with those who fear
Him, and He will show them His covenant.*

(PSALM 25:14)

The idea of marriage came out of God's heart; it was designed by Him, and we know that whatever God creates is always "good." In the Garden of Eden, Adam was lonely, and God made him a mate, Eve, and started the covenant of marriage. As our Creator, God knows how to improve good marriages and rebuild bad ones. God's Word is His instruction manual, and from it we can learn the keys to a successful marriage.

Key 1: Make God the third person in your relationship. Ecclesiastes 4:12 says, *"Though one may be overpowered by another, two can withstand him. And a threefold cord is not quickly broken."* God is the third element in an unbreakable marriage. When your marriage begins to fray or unravel like a cord, God can weave your relationship back together again. He will help you up when you're down, warm your heart with hope when all seems lost, and stand with you against anything or anyone who would try to destroy your marriage and home. Commit your marriage to God; ask for His help and guidance; and seek His wisdom—in prayer and in His Word.

Key 2: Consider your marriage a covenant. Malachi 2:14 says, *"Because the LORD has been witness between you and the wife of your youth, . . . she is your companion and your wife by covenant."* As a Christian, you are in a covenant relationship with God. He never leaves you alone. He is with you even when you aren't aware of Him, when you feel awful, or when you do things wrong. Marriage is also a covenant relationship, which means you are fully committed to your mate "in sickness and in health," and in hard times and abundance.

Key 3: Covenants are based on sacrifice. Jesus's very life was a sacrifice for our sins. In the same way, a marriage relationship is based upon a sacrificial covenant. The only way to put life into a dying marriage is for you to die to yourself and your selfish desires. Understand your spouse's needs and look for ways to meet them despite your own desires.

Marriage is about giving. If both partners are focused on meeting the other's needs, each will get all their needs met in a greater way than they could have ever imagined.

Key 4: Let God put your marriage in order because He created the divine order. He can bind you together into a into a threefold cord, with each having a role. The wife's role is to support and encourage. What pleased the husband of the Proverbs 31 woman the most was that she supported and encouraged him. God called wives to praise their husbands. God designed the husband's role in marriage to protect and provide for his wife. This makes a woman feel safe and secure. A man of God has a special, unique glory because of his wife. First Corinthians 11:7 says, *"For a man indeed ought not to cover his head, since he is the image and glory of God; but woman is the glory of man."* The wife gets glory from God and her husband.

God wants His people to understand covenant relationship: *"The secret of the LORD is with those who fear Him, and He will show them His covenant"* (Psalm 25:14). If you regard God as the third person in your marriage, He will show you the secret of a covenant marriage and guide you in making your marriage fantastic!

Untangling Twisted Relationships

When a man's ways please the LORD, he makes
even his enemies to be at peace with him.

(PROVERBS 16:7)

D o you know why the devil likes broken relationships? Do you know why there is so much strife between husbands and wives, mothers and daughters, fathers and sons? It's because when the devil can twist relationships and keep Christians from agreeing in prayer, he can stop them from moving in power to fulfill God's will on the earth!

Jesus said, *"If two of you agree on earth concerning anything that they ask, it will be done for them by My Father in heaven"* (Matthew 18:19). Things begin to transpire when two Christians get in harmony— anything they agree upon concerning heaven and earth will happen.

Are there some relationships in your life that need healing? Are you tangled in any relationships that need to be broken? Your heavenly Father has provided a way to untangle twisted relationships and bring order, harmony, and blessing into this important aspect of your life.

Let's look at Jacob and Esau's twisted relationship and discover how God's people were able to unravel some pretty sticky situations. Do you recall the story in Genesis 27 about how Jacob stole the family blessing from his brother Esau? Once Esau discovered how Jacob had tricked his dad into giving Jacob the blessing (a very important matter in those days), Esau burned with hatred for Jacob—to the point of wanting to kill him!

Their relationship was broken, and Jacob ran for his life—right into another bad situation. He went to his mother's family, where he married two of his uncle's daughters. When we marry, we don't get to choose our in-laws. Now I know that you have never had any in-law problems, but I'll bet you know someone who has. It just so happens that Jacob had a rotten

father-in-law. I don't believe that anyone has had a worse in-law than Jacob had. You can read about all the bad things he did to Jacob in Genesis 29 and 30. The situation finally got so bad that, about 20 years later, God spoke to Jacob in a dream and told him to leave: *"Arise, get out of this land, and return to the land of your family"* (Genesis 31:13). Sometimes, God's solution to a problematic relationship is to sever that association. If you are involved in an ungodly or unhealthy relationship, God may separate you from them.

But returning home meant he had to face up to his twisted relationship with Esau. What could he do to make it right? He prayed. Genesis 32:24 tells us about the time when Jacob was "left alone" with God; that prayer meeting was the turning point in Jacob's life and relationships.

You and I need to spend time alone with God if we are to put our relationships right. Allow God to talk to you personally. Most twisted relationships can be healed when you are willing to let God change *you* rather than expecting the other person to change.

Proverbs 16:7 says, *"When a man's ways please the LORD, he makes even his enemies to be at peace with him."* Once our hearts are right, God will make our relationships right! The same God who untangled Jacob and Esau's broken relationship can perform a miracle for you.

Harmony in Our Homes

"Whatever you bind on earth will be bound in heaven, and whatever you loose on earth will be loosed in heaven."
(MATTHEW 18:18)

Anyone who reads Hannah's story in 1 Samuel can't help but feel sorry for her. Hannah had no children and was the object of ridicule and scorn from her husband's second wife, Peninnah. Hannah took the only route out of her suffering and the only way out of her bitter relationship with Peninnah—she prayed.

Hannah prayed before the Lord, and she *"wept in anguish"* (1 Samuel 1:10). This was obviously an intense time of prayer for Hannah. Notice *how* she prayed and what happened next: *"Now Hannah spoke in her heart; only her lips moved, but her voice was not heard. Therefore Eli thought she was drunk"* (1 Samuel 1:13). Hannah could have become offended and said, "Well, if Eli, the priest, doesn't understand my heart, I'll never come into the tabernacle of God again!" But if the devil could have made her offended over Eli's words, Hannah never would have gotten what she desired most—a son. Hannah stayed in faith, she shared her burden with Eli, and God granted her prayer. You never read about a bad relationship between Hannah and Peninnah after the birth of Samuel. I believe their relationship was healed because Hannah sought the Lord instead of becoming bitter and hostile toward those around her. If you and I are going to see victories in our relationships, we are going to have to pray in earnest.

Often, binding and loosing must take place before unity develops. Jesus taught His disciples: *"Whatever you bind on earth will be bound in heaven, and whatever you loose on earth will be loosed in heaven"* (Matthew 18:18). If we are going to have harmonious relationships with our spouses, our fellow employees, and our relatives, we need to learn the value of binding and loosing, just like my mother did. After she was saved and Spirit-filled, she could hardly wait to tell her family about Jesus. One year, all summer, our out-of-state relatives came to visit, but the next summer, nobody came! All the relatives were turned off by her witnessing. My mother quickly

learned about binding and loosing. She bound the devil from working in her family, and she loosed God to speak to each and every one of them about His Son, Jesus. The Lord heard those binding-and-loosing prayers, and almost every one of my mother's siblings was saved—and their children soon followed. Praise the Lord! Binding-and-loosing prayers will pave the way for agreement and unity with your relatives.

Sometimes we may not know what God's will is concerning a person or a situation. Those are the times when we need to pray in the Spirit and allow God to reveal His will to us. Romans 8:26 says: *"We do not know what we should pray for as we ought, but the Spirit Himself makes intercession for us with groanings which cannot be uttered."* We may not know what to pray, but the Holy Spirit knows how to pray the kinds of prayers that untangle the toughest "knots" in our relationships.

Are there some twisted areas in your life that need this kind of prayer in the Spirit? A hurt relationship with a spouse, child, relative, or someone else? Spend some time praying in the Spirit for any seemingly "hard cases." Allow God to work through those relationships and bring harmony and unity into your home.

Raising 21st-Century Heroes

Train up a child in the way he should go, and
when he is old he will not depart from it.
(PROVERBS 22:6)

We have grown so accustomed to the evils around us, we scarcely notice them. It's not until the monstrous crosses over and affects the mundane that we see it, and tragedy can pierce our heart in these perilous times.

These are difficult days for parents and even more challenging days for our youth. The world does not embrace biblical principles or a Christian lifestyle. Satan diligently promotes a pervasive system of immorality that brings constant, unbending pressure to bear upon the souls of our young people. Sadly, many have fallen in the face of such opposition.

However, that is not the whole story. God's power is far greater than the power of the enemy. Every day, more and more young people are drawing the line and choosing God's camp, whatever the cost. Some, like Columbine victims Cassie Bernall and Rachel Scott, are known for their martyrdom. We hear of young military personnel who touch our hearts with their bravery. Many others wouldn't be recognized in the next town. They have become known as good soldiers in God's army of young believers—shining stars who reflect the image of the loving God who created them.

What separates these heroes from their peers? Why do some young people take the high road when the low road is so easy to ride? I believe the answer is simply "truth." Armed with the truth, these young heroes are ready to face whatever comes their way. Their hearts are stocked with enough "ammunition" to sustain them in the defining moments that come to every young life.

Parents are strategically placed in authority over their children with this end in mind—to *"train up a child in the way he should go, and when he is old he will not depart from it"* (Proverbs 22:6). The parent is, by divine design, the primary truth-giver in a child's life. As a parent, you have the God-given power, authority, and ability to help form the character of a 21st-century hero.

I realize the enormity of that statement. Given godly guidance, love, and direction, your child can grow to be strong in the Lord, immovable, and a world-changer. To be successfully used as an instrument of God to accomplish this task, you must demonstrate the character of a good soldier to your child. There will be moments when tough love is the only way to victory— times when it would be easier to give in than to act in true love. There is no easy way to grow godly character. We can't let nature take its course, lest our children grow up to become 21st-century adults who fit Paul's distressing description in 2 Timothy 3:1–5:

In the last days . . . men will be lovers of themselves, lovers of money, boasters, proud, blasphemers, disobedient to parents, unthankful, unholy, unloving, unforgiving, slanderers, without self-control, brutal, despisers of good, traitors, headstrong, haughty, lovers of pleasure rather than lovers of God, having a form of godliness but denying its power.

No, no, no! That is not for my children nor yours! God has better plans for your children. Stick with His Word and stick by your child. Be consistent in both the small issues and the big deals. Demonstrate your conviction and your reliance on God. Mentor your children for success by speaking the truth in love over and over again. Don't grow weary of doing the right thing. Arm your children with the truth. Keep pressing in, investing in their destinies, and you will raise real heroes for the 21st century.

Farmer God

God's Domino Effect

*"Believe on the Lord Jesus Christ, and you
will be saved, you and your household."*

(ACTS 16:31)

Did you know that when God called you into His kingdom, He called your household too, and that one person's faith can lead to generations of believers? Throughout the Bible, you see God's concern for families. He wants your family to be saved and blessed.

The Bible is full of examples of whole household salvation. Starting in Genesis, God shows His concern not just for individuals but for families. He told Noah to take his family into the ark (see Genesis 7:1). In Genesis 17:2, Abraham entered into an everlasting covenant with God, and we see that God's promises also extended to succeeding generations. God marked Abraham's family and all his seed after him and called them to be His people.

Moses is proof of his parents' faith for their children's salvation. Hebrews 11:23 says that Moses's parents hid him and set him aside. They marked him by faith as a covenant child—a child who was a part of their household's salvation. And God used Moses to deliver His entire nation and people out of Egypt. Exodus 12:3, 7 says, *"Every man shall take for himself a lamb, . . . a lamb for a household. And they shall take some of the blood and put it on the two doorposts and on the lintel of the houses where they eat it."* God delivered the whole family by the blood of a lamb. Likewise, God provided Jesus Christ, not just for us, but for our family—the Lamb of God set aside for household salvation. That includes your children, regardless of their age. Claim them as covenant children and let God use them to do His work.

Jesus blessed the household of Zacchaeus—someone most people wanted to avoid. But Jesus said, *"Today salvation has come to this house, because he also is a son of Abraham"* (Luke 19:9). In Acts 16:31, Paul tells the Philippian jailer: *"Believe on the Lord Jesus Christ, and you will be saved, you and your household."* Both Zacchaeus and the jailer, and their households, needed God and were born-again. God wants families united in tender, loving relationships within His great big family.

When Lydia, a businesswoman, met Paul down by a river, she didn't know that she would be the key to open Europe to the gospel. But when God opened her heart, she opened her house; and when she opened her house, God used her family to open a continent (see Acts 16:13–15). You may be the only believer in your home, but look to Lydia as an example.

When Cornelius came to the Lord, he and his household were saved and Spirit-filled (see Acts 10). Acts also tells us that the promise of the outpouring of the Holy Spirit is *"to you and to your children, and to all who are afar off, as many as the Lord our God will call"* (Acts 2:39). God wants generations of Spirit-filled believers.

Don't ever think somebody is too hard for the Lord to save. A young man in our church was able to lead his hardened father to the Lord after much prayer. Even those who seem impossible in our eyes are a cinch for God. You can be the one God uses to lead your loved ones to the Lord. One believer can lead to another—that's God's "domino effect." One believer is all it takes because God has promised to pour out His Spirit on your family. Just trust Him.

Household Blessings

*"You shall rejoice in all to which you have put
your hand, you and your households, in which
the LORD your God has blessed you."*

(DEUTERONOMY 12:7)

Once your family has made Jesus the head of the household, God can begin to use your family for His work. Just as each of us is set aside for something special in God's kingdom, God sets aside families, too. God has an appointment for you, your children, and your household. For example, Aaron's family was set apart in a unique way. Exodus 29:9 says that Aaron and his sons were set aside as a perpetual priesthood. God anointed Aaron, and that anointing flowed to his children and all succeeding generations. The Levitical priesthood was a family thing. If you follow the Lord, your anointing can flow from you to your children, to your grandchildren, and down through the generations.

There are also blessings connected with household salvation. God blessed Obed-Edom's home when the Ark, the presence of God, was left at his house (see 2 Samuel 6:11–12). Whenever the presence of God resides in a family, that whole family is blessed. One of those blessings is joy. Deuteronomy 12:7 talks about rejoicing in the home: *"And there... you shall rejoice in all to which you have put your hand, you and your households, in which the L*ORD* your God has blessed you."* Your house should be a place of rejoicing, where you can have fun and be delighted with one another. Rejoicing is important because *"the joy of the L*ORD* is your strength"* (Nehemiah 8:10). If you are a child of God, you can claim the blessing of joy in your home today. Rejoice and let His joy fill your house from attic to basement!

God not only wants rejoicing in your house, He wants healing. Jesus healed the son of a nobleman who wasn't even a Jew. The nobleman turned to Jesus for help, and Jesus told him that his son would live: *"The father knew that it was at the*

same hour in which Jesus said to him, 'Your son lives.' And he himself believed, and his whole household" (John 4:53). A father believed his son was healed, and the whole household was blessed through the faith of the father—his whole household received life. There is healing for your household, too, if you will follow Jesus and believe the truth.

The Lord also blesses us with peace. Luke 10:5–6 says, *"Whatever house you enter, first say, 'Peace to this house.' And if a son of peace is there, your peace will rest on it; if not, it will return to you."* Pray over your house; believe that instead of discord, there will be peace in your home. If you welcome Jesus into your home, then peace and love will abide there, too.

Paul also prayed a blessing of mercy on the house of Onesiphorus: *"The Lord grant mercy to the household of Onesiphorus, for he often refreshed me"* (2 Timothy 1:16). Mercy is so important because without mercy, it's not a home; it's just a house. We need mercy at home more than anyplace else. Ephesians 2:6 says we are seated in heavenly places in Christ Jesus. And Jesus sits on the mercy seat! So should we. If you sow mercy with your family, you can create an atmosphere of acceptance that turns a house into a home!

Why not pray and ask God what His ambition is for your household? Then wait for His direction. Pray that God's will be done. Then let the Holy Spirit take over and see the blessings flow.

Worship:
Your Spiritual Antenna

Let us continually offer the sacrifice of praise to God,
that is, the fruit of our lips, giving thanks to His name.
(HEBREWS 13:15)

You can set an atmosphere for the Holy Spirit to talk to you. When you hear from the Holy Spirit, you get God's answers for the situations in your life. The Holy Spirit, the Spirit of truth, transmits the overcoming victory of Jesus into you. Your job is to tune into the Holy Spirit by offering up worship, developing your spiritual perception, and building up your human spirit by praying in tongues.

You can't hear His voice when you're listening to other voices. You can't receive a call from God if you're busy taking a call from your emotions. Your emotions can keep you from hearing Him. One of the emotions that shouts the loudest is fear. When fear, worry, anxiety, or depression dominate your thinking, they block out the still, small voice of the Spirit. Hang up on fear! The Word says to cast all that on Jesus because He cares for you (see 1 Peter 5:7).

Ambition can also hinder your reception of His voice. Maybe you're a doer, a driver, or an over-achiever. There's nothing wrong with wanting to be successful, but if that drive dominates your thoughts, you won't be able to clearly hear the voice of the Spirit. The pursuit of pleasure, selfishness, and failure to deal with problems also hinder His voice.

To tune into Him, tune out everything else, and focus on things of the Spirit. One way to clean out the clutter of your mind is to worship God. It increases your sensitivity to the voice of the Spirit and helps you focus your attention on God; it causes your problems and desires to fade into the background. Worship is something you do, not something that happens to you. Sometimes, worship can even be a "sacrifice of praise": *"Let us continually offer the sacrifice of praise to God, that is, the fruit of our lips, giving thanks to His name"* (Hebrews 13:15). Look at David. He understood, cherished, and delighted in the Holy Spirit the most of any Old Testament character. He was a master of worship, a singer of praise, and one who reveled in worshiping God. He didn't want to lose his sweet communion with the Holy Spirit.

Worship is your spiritual antenna. As you worship God, you will begin to develop spiritual perception/reception. Perception is one of the ways the Holy Spirit will communicate

to you. You may not often hear Him with your ears, but you can perceive what He's saying as He whispers truth to your spirit. (See Luke 8:46; 9:47.)

Praying in tongues is another way to heighten your communication with the Holy Spirit. First Corinthians 14:2, 4 says, *"For he who speaks in a tongue does not speak to men but to God, . . . He who speaks in a tongue edifies himself, but he who prophesies edifies the church."* To "edify" means to "build up." Praying in tongues not only builds you up but also strengthens, rebuilds, and recharges your spirit so you can hear the Holy Spirit more clearly.

The Holy Spirit has all the answers. When you face a dilemma or a decision, don't reason in your heart; instead, worship and pray in the Spirit, and you can receive the answers you need.

Listening and Obeying

"Behold, to obey is better than sacrifice,
and to heed than the fat of rams."

(1 SAMUEL 15:22)

When God speaks to us, He always has a purpose. God wants to maintain open communication with you, so don't hang up on Him! If you tell God, "No," too often, He may just stop talking to you. God warns us not to turn away from that voice: *"See to it that you do not refuse him who speaks. If they did not escape when they refused him who warned them on earth, how much less will we, if we turn away from him who warns us from heaven?"* (Hebrews 12:25 NIV).

One of the most important aspects of a Christian's walk with God is the ability to hear His voice and then obey it. God has reasons why He wants us to know His voice. Scripture gives many instances of people and nations responding to the voice of God, beginning with Adam and Eve. Genesis 3:8 tells us that Adam and Eve heard God's voice in the garden. God gave them dominion over all the earth, and He talked to them as He prepared them for that responsibility.

God addressed the nation of Israel because He wanted the Israelites to carry His Word to the world—to prepare the world for its coming Messiah. God gave the Ten Commandments to the nation of Israel—not just to Moses—because He planned on sending the Messiah through Israel. God still wants His people to carry his Word and the knowledge of the Messiah to the world.

God told Saul, the first king of Israel, to *completely* destroy Amalek. Saul listened and conquered the Amalekites—his way. He spared their king and kept the best of the plunder. Samuel then confronted Saul and told him that God had rejected him as king for his failure to obey: *"Behold, to obey is better than sacrifice, and to heed than the fat of rams"* (1 Samuel 15:22).

Perhaps no one else in the Old Testament knew the voice of God better than David—he knew God's voice so well that he heard the Father and the Son talking to each other! (See Psalm 2 and 110.) Reinforced and encouraged by God's Word, David became a mighty leader and king of Israel. Not only that, but God promised David that He would send the Messiah through

David's line of descendants. Now, don't think David was God's pet! He was human, just like the rest of us. The difference was that David *listened* to God and *obeyed* Him.

God continued to illustrate His purposes for communicating with men and women in the New Testament. When Martha complained to Jesus that her sister Mary wasn't helping her, Jesus pointed out the importance of hearing God's voice: *"There is really only one thing worth being concerned about. Mary has discovered it—and I won't take it away from her!"* (Luke 10:42 TLB). What was that "one thing"? Mary had learned to sit at Jesus's feet and hear His voice.

In Philippians 3:10, Paul said his goal in life was to know Christ. You can't really know someone unless you learn to recognize that person's voice. There's no doubt that Paul really knew the Lord—his 13 New Testament books give us many details about Christ and how to walk and talk with God. Explore these people's lives so that you can also learn to hear and obey His voice.

Farmer God

*"I chose you and appointed you that you should go
and bear fruit, and that your fruit should remain."*
(JOHN 15:16)

There is something about being sensitive to the voice of God that has to do with your intimate relationship with Him. When you begin to love Him and listen to His voice, you're going to produce fruit because love always creates: *"I chose you and appointed you that you should go and bear fruit, and that your fruit should remain"* (John 15:16).

So why aren't we more creative? Why aren't we producing more? Isaiah said it's because we don't listen enough:

> *Listen to me, listen as I plead: Does a farmer always
> plow and never sow? Is he forever harrowing the
> soil and never planting it? Does he not finally plant
> his many kinds of grain, each in its own section
> of his land? He knows just what to do, for God has
> made him see and understand.* **(ISAIAH 28:23–26 TLB)**

God prepares you to listen in many ways; He prepares your heart to listen to what He has to say to you. He also gives you seed in your heart, and when you obey Him, you bring forth the harvest He wants. Yet He tells different things to different people because we are not all alike. He has "many kinds of grain," and we are planted in different places. He prepares *you* for what He has for *you*.

When He speaks, He "threshes" what He gives you and harvests it in a most unique way:

> *He doesn't thresh all grains the same. A sledge is*
> *never used on dill, but it is beaten with a stick.*
> *A threshing wheel is never rolled on cumin, but*
> *it is beaten softly with a flail. Bread grain is easily*
> *crushed, so he doesn't keep on pounding it.*
> *The Lord Almighty is a wonderful teacher and*
> *gives the farmer wisdom.* (ISAIAH 28:27–29 TLB)

God uses different threshing tools on us. In the same way that dill is too fragile to use a sledge on, some people are too fragile, so He uses a little stick because that is what it will take to get their attention. At other times, He may use a flail because He wants us to be the seasoning in someone's life—sometimes we're the dill and sometimes we're the cumin.

God might use a stick, a flail, a sledge, or even a wheel to get your attention. But remember, God always has a purpose in what He tells you. God's ultimate reason for speaking to you is to encourage you to be a "farmer" just like He is. He wants you to go forth and bring forth fruit, and for your fruit to remain. Once you know what God wants you to do, you must obey. Even when it looks like you're failing, God can still use you to "season" the people around you. After all, just a little dill added to cucumbers makes great pickles!

God's Vision for Your Future

*For I know the thoughts that I think toward
you, says the Lord, thoughts of peace and not
of evil, to give you a future and a hope.*

(JEREMIAH 29:11)

Whether you are 19 or 91, God has a vision for your life that you need to fulfill. That vision will make it possible for you to wake up every day knowing what He wants from you instead of guessing what you should do.

You may think, *God doesn't have anything planned for me. I'm not intelligent, talented, pretty, or spiritual enough to be used by God.* Satan is the one who tells you those lies. God's truth is clearly spelled out in Jeremiah 29:11: *"For I know the thoughts that I think toward you, says the Lord, thoughts of peace and not of evil, to give you a future and a hope."* God's "future and a

hope," or vision for your life, does not include pain, suffering, or poverty—those are the devil's plans for you. God envisions you experiencing peace and knowing your purpose.

You may think, *That may be true for other people, but I'm always messing up. God's mad at me because I blow it all the time. I haven't been tithing. I haven't been reading my Bible and praying as I should. I have been cold towards Him. So, if God has any plans for my life, I bet they are bad. He wants to pay me back for all the bad things I've done.* That is wrong thinking because, as a child of God, He called you to achieve wonderful things even before He created you!

If you want to catch God's vision, ask the Holy Spirit to show it to you. The Holy Spirit causes people to dream dreams of their future and have visions of God's goals for their lives. Don't become discouraged if the vision isn't revealed right away. Wait on God! *"And you will seek Me and find Me, when you search for Me with all your heart"* (Jeremiah 29:13).

God's vision will give you direction. Knowing where you're supposed to go and what you're supposed to do is important because it will give you confidence and strength to keep pursuing the goal. *"Where there is no vision, the people perish"* (Proverbs 29:18 KJV). Without God's vision, you won't achieve the things you need in order to fulfill His purpose for you.

It seems to me like even the apostle Paul lost his way when he didn't wait for God's leading. Although his first missionary journey produced signs and wonders and a crop of new churches, he nearly flopped on his second journey because doors of opportunity kept slamming in his face. Maybe he hadn't waited for God to tell him where to go. But then, one night, he dreamt of a man asking him to come to Macedonia; he finally received the direction he needed (see Acts 16). When he followed that vision, God blessed him by opening Europe to the gospel.

When God gives you a vision for your life, follow it. If you're not doing what God wants you to do, you will be unhappy and frustrated. When you do what God wants, your dreams will come true. Trust in the Lord and delight in His plans and goals for you so He can give you the desires of your heart (Psalm 37:3–4). Then you will have godly success.

Just Say, "Yes"

*For all the promises of God in Him are Yes, and in
Him Amen, to the glory of God through us.*

(2 CORINTHIANS 1:20)

What if God told you to build a ship in your front yard? Would you say, "Yes," or would you say, "Oh, Lord, what about my neighbors? What would they think? What would they do? People will ridicule me. I would get in trouble. Where will I get the time and the materials? Why did you pick *me* to do this, Lord?"

Noah may have thought these same things. Yet, in the long run, he said, "Yes, Lord, I will do this thing you ask." Even when his neighbors laughed at him and ridiculed him, Noah kept saying, "Yes, Lord. It doesn't make sense for me to build a ship when I've never seen rain or floods, but I will do as you ask." And when the

waters came, whom did God save? Whom did He bless? Whom did God make the new father of the human race? It was the man who said, "Yes."

If you knew that saying "Yes" to God would make a world of difference in your life, would you say it? If you were told that the desires of your heart, the answers to your problems, and miracles for your health and finances could happen if you said "Yes," would you say it? Then say it! Just say "Yes!"

Notice in 2 Corinthians 1:20 that when God gave us His promises, He meant them to be for always and for all people who would claim them: *"For all the promises of God in Him are Yes, and in Him Amen, to the glory of God through us."* The only way you can claim His promises is to say, "Yes," to God. Notice, too, that this scripture also says His promises are *"yes and amen through us"*; nothing will come to pass **until** you utter that second, "Yes."

The only thing you had to do to receive God's miracle-gift of salvation was to say, "Yes, I believe Jesus is my Savior, and, yes, I accept Him into my heart." You said, "Yes." Receiving the rest of God's promises is just as easy. All you have to do to receive His blessing, to receive the desires of your heart, to change circumstances, is to just say, "Yes," to God.

All of us have bad circumstances. If you say "Yes" to your circumstances instead of "Yes" to the Word, your circumstances are going to overwhelm you. But if you say "Yes" to the Word, you're going to overwhelm your circumstances.

Now, this is important! You must be sure you are saying "Yes" to what God says and "No" to what the devil says—that is, say, "No" to the circumstances, "No" to your flesh, fears, and doubts. If you say "yes" to your circumstances, you're saying "yes" to the devil. You must agree with God. You must say, "Yes," to the life, and that is Jesus Christ. He said, *"I am the way, the truth, and the life"* (John 14:6). He said, *"I am come that they might have life, and that they might have it more abundantly"* (John 10:10 KJV).

When you say "Yes" to His "Yes," then you get His life, so just say, "Yes"!

What's in Your Hands?

"See, I have engraved you on the palms of my hands."
(ISAIAH 49:16 NIV)

*I*f you've given your heart to the Lord, your name is carved into God's hands; *"See, I have engraved you on the palms of my hands"* (Isaiah 49:16 NIV). He doesn't just write your name in pencil or ink that can be washed away when you make a mistake. No! God *carved* your name into His hands. That's how serious God is about His relationship with you. Your hands are the hands of a winner! God has put the talents, abilities, anointing, and resources into your hands that will cause you to be wonderfully successful—if you'll allow Him to direct your life.

God has given us the most precious thing in His hands—His only begotten son, Jesus, our Savior. How can we give Him any less than our best? Christians are the hands and feet of Jesus on Earth today. Look at your hands. Regardless of your income, age, education level, gender, ethnicity, or race, God has put in your hands everything you need to fulfill your destiny. You have winning hands because *"Christ in you,* [is] *the hope of glory"*

(Colossians 1:27). Everyone is born with certain talents and abilities. Then, when we are born-again, we receive an anointing and God's direction to make the maximum use of our gifts.

During his college years, former Chinese leader Jiang Zemin participated in a student movement in China against Chiang Kai-shek. After being wounded in a skirmish, he ended up in the hospital with a Christian nurse. She read to him daily from the book of John. When relating this story to a Christian leader, Jiang said, "I came to love the Gospel of John," and then asked for a good translation to read. Think about that Christian nurse. She only had nursing abilities in her hands, yet look at how God used her. When she gave those abilities to God, she was able to minister physically and spiritually to the man who would become a future president of China (1993–2003). What could God do with what you have in your hands?

Hannah was unable to have children. She cried out to God in prayer and declared, "If you give me a son, (put a son in my hand), I will give him back to you" (see 1 Samuel 1:1–2:26).

God heard her prayer, and Samuel was conceived. Samuel became a judge, high priest, and prophet—a man who changed the course of Israel's history. He anointed Saul and then David as

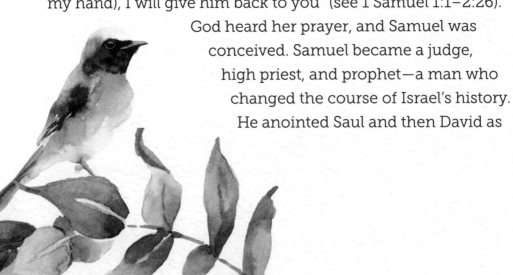

kings and wrote 1 and 2 Samuel. When Hannah gave what was in her hand, she gave a great blessing to God's people, and God gave her a beautiful, prophetic song (1 Samuel 2:1–10) and five additional children.

The destinies of your children are in your hands. The way you raise them and pray for them can determine their future. Regardless of their age, you can give them to God. A former drug dealer was saved in a Billy Graham meeting. God cleaned him up inside and out; he eventually came to work for our ministry and became one of our top executives. He became a tremendously successful businessman. What happened? His born-again Methodist mother believed that God would deliver her son. She refused to let go of her faith until his deliverance came to pass. If you have a child who isn't living for the Lord, regardless of their age, that son or daughter is in your hands. Give them to the Lord, right now. Reach out your hands to God and pray with me: "Father, I believe the children you've put in my hand have a destiny to live for and serve you. I give them to you and believe that your destiny will come to pass for my children. Amen."

You may have things in your hands that God wants to use for His kingdom and glory. God's hands are outstretched to you, and He wants to use you for the good of one or many. Let Him direct you and watch what He does through you!

Vessels

Make Your Calling and Election Sure

Therefore, brethren, be even more diligent to make your call and election sure, for if you do these things you will never stumble.

(2 PETER 1:10)

Your heavenly Father has big dreams for you that reveal the ministry He has ordained for you. You may think, "I'm not in the ministry!" Think again! The word "ministry" means "to serve or to aid." Any service you perform for Jesus is your ministry, and God has ordained specific works for you to accomplish: *"For we are His workmanship, created in Christ Jesus for good works, which God prepared beforehand that we should walk in them"* (Ephesians 2:10).

Second Peter 1:10 reveals two essential requirements for fruitful ministry and the manifestation of God's spiritual dream for you: *"Therefore, brethren, be even more diligent to make your call and election sure, for if you do these things you will never stumble"* (2 Peter 1:10). Your ministry has two parts—a calling and an election.

Both your calling and election relate to your ministry. Your calling has to do with your ministry to others. Your election relates to your ministry to the Lord. Jesus told two parables that help explain the differences between these two facets of ministry. In Matthew 25, we read about the parable of the talents, which relates to your *calling.* In Luke 19, we read about the parable of the pounds, which relates to your *election.* (Because there is so much to this, we will explore these for the next two days.)

In the parable of the pounds (Luke 19:11–27 KJV), we read about 10 pounds distributed equally among 10 servants. The parallel in the spiritual life is that no person receives more of the new birth than any other; every person gets the same amount of total salvation when they are born-again. That is your election.

In the parable of the talents (Matthew 25:14–30), distribution was not the same for each person. One man received five talents, another received two, and another received one. As it relates to calling, some people have so many talents that it is truly amazing: they sing, operate in gifts of healing, preach, and teach. They receive several talents through which God wants to work. In the parable, these talents were all distributed by a man;

the gifts and talents of Christians are distributed by the Holy Spirit: *"But the manifestation of the Spirit is given to each one for the profit of all"* (1 Corinthians 12:7).

God's dream for you involves the use of the talents and gifts He has given to you. The apostle Peter said it this way: *"As each one has received a gift, minister it to one another, as good stewards of the manifold grace of God"* (1 Peter 4:10). We know from 2 Corinthians 4:7 that we are earthen vessels to be used by God on this earth. Just as vessels are used to pour forth their contents, your talents were placed within you for the very purpose of being poured out to meet the needs of others. That is true ministry, and there's no expiration date on your ministry.

Think of the ways you can be a vessel poured out to help others. If you're a good cook, take some meals to a homebound person. If you can repair cars, help a widow or single mom get her car fixed. Pray about it. You'll be surprised at how God shows you to use your talents.

Earthen Vessels

*But we have this treasure in earthen vessels, that the
excellence of the power may be of God and not of us.*
(2 CORINTHIANS 4:7)

Many Christians today want God to put them into a place of authority, but they refuse to exercise the single pound (talent) that God has given them (see Luke 19:11–27 KJV). They are content with the status quo. At church, they may shout, "Hallelujah! Praise the Lord!" but at work, they hide their Christianity in a napkin so that no one receives the ministry of the Holy Spirit through them.

Your relationship with the Lord will grow if you are daily in His Word, if you pray in the Spirit, if you fellowship with other believers, and if you choose to be used by Him. It is vital that you esteem your election to God and develop it: *"But we have this treasure in earthen vessels, that the excellence of the power may be of God and not of us"* (2 Corinthians 4:7). When you do that, you will find that ministering your talents will come easily and naturally. You will find yourself pouring forth from your vessel to others and fulfilling God's dream for you!

The biggest obstacle standing in the way of believers ministering in God's fullness is the idea that one talent or one pound can't make a significant contribution. I believe that the story of Elisha and the widow, recorded in 2 Kings 4, is God's way of showing us that it is important to use what little we have. This desperate widow's husband had died, and the creditors were about to take her sons away as payment for her debt! She cried to Elisha to do something which would reverse the situation, and Elisha replied, "What do you have?"

The answer to any problem starts with what we already have! Elisha took what the woman already had—a little bit of oil—and God multiplied it until there was enough to sell it and pay off her debt.

That is what God wants you to do with the talent He has given to you—begin using what "little bit" you have so that He can multiply it to meet your needs and the needs of others around you. Like the widow, you must find some empty vessels (friends, neighbors, co-workers), start pouring forth what you have, and watch God increase your ministry and give you greater authority at home, at work, and at church.

God's dream for you will only become a reality as you diligently make your calling and election sure. Pray with me now, and start *today* to pour forth your talents in ministry to others:

> Dear heavenly Father, thank you for the salvation you provided through your Son, Jesus Christ. I want to take what I already have and use it to bless myself and others. Rather than hiding my ministry, I want to begin pouring forth what I have to fulfill your dream for me. In Jesus's name, amen.

Becoming a Faithful Servant

"Well done, good and faithful servant; you were faithful over a few things, I will make you ruler over many things. Enter into the joy of your lord."

(MATTHEW 25:21)

I n Matthew 25:14, the kingdom of heaven is likened to a man (God) preparing for a journey and delivering his goods in varied amounts to his servants (us). Next, we're told what happened during this man's absence: *"Then he who had received the five talents went and traded with them, and made another five talents. And likewise he who had received two gained two more also. But he who had received one went and dug in the ground, and hid his lord's money"* (Matthew 25:16–18).

When the master returned, there was a day of reckoning: *"So he who had received five talents came and brought five other talents, saying, 'Lord, you delivered to me five talents; look, I have gained five more talents besides them'"* (Matthew 25:20). Here was someone who poured out his talents.By using what he was given, he multiplied what he had. Notice his master's response: *"His lord said to him, 'Well done, good and faithful servant; you were faithful over a few things, I will make you ruler over many things. Enter into the joy of your lord'"* (Matthew 25:21).

There is a joy you get from ministering to others. But some Christians are constantly grumpy because they aren't fulfilling God's dream for their lives. These believers aren't being the vessels He ordained them to be—as was the case of the man who received one talent: *"Then he who had received the one talent came and said, 'Lord, I knew you to be a hard man, . . .' And I was afraid, and went and hid your talent in the ground"* (Matthew 25:24–25). Because the servant hid his talent, his master said, *"You wicked and lazy servant, . . . take the talent from him, and give it to him who has ten talents"* (Matthew 25:26, 28).

Luke 19 records the story of a nobleman who went to a far country to receive a kingdom and then returned. Before he left, he gave each of his 10 servants one pound and said, "Occupy until I return." Each servant had just one pound; each Christian receives an equal opportunity to develop his relationship with the Lord. Just as in the lesson of the talents, the importance of each pound was in what was done with it. Every born-again believer has the same rights and privileges in respect to growing in faith and growing in the knowledge of God. The question is: what have you done with what you have?

In this parable, the first servant said, "I multiplied the one pound I had; now it's ten pounds!" The nobleman was so pleased that he gave the good servant *"authority over ten cities"* (Luke 19:17 KJV). Likewise, the second servant received authority over five cities for having multiplied his pound five times. Another servant, however, came to the nobleman and said, "I hid my pound in a napkin." This man didn't want to do anything wrong, so he did nothing at all! He was satisfied to maintain the status quo. The master took away what little he had, saying, *"I say to you, that to everyone who has will be given; and from him who does not have, even what he has will be taken away from him"* (Luke 19:26).

We feel good pouring out the talents God gives us, because that's why they were given to us in the first place. Many times, we are envious of those who have many talents; we feel that our single talent isn't worth using. But it is only through using what you have, whether it's one talent or 10, that God can multiply and bless your ministry.

Realizing Your Potential

The effective, fervent prayer of a
righteous man avails much.

(JAMES 5:16)

I heard of a famous surgeon who once said that if he had only four minutes to perform a lifesaving operation, he would spend one whole minute just planning his course of action! Planning our work and working our plan will help all of us achieve more in our personal and family lives and help us accomplish more for the Lord. I believe the Bible provides some keys to helping us experience God's full potential for our lives, and I want to share them with you.

Every plan's success depends on prayer. We can set 100 goals, but they will never come to pass if we don't pray and get the power of God's Word behind them. Make a list of your goals,

and pray over them daily. Constantly remind God and yourself of what it is you desire. By praying daily, you've put yourself in agreement with James 5:16 that says, *"The effective, fervent prayer of a righteous man avails much."* Your plans will avail much if they are supported by daily prayer.

Even the worthiest goal or objective is impossible to reach without some intermediate steps leading up to it. Trust God to give you the little steps that you need in order to reach your goals. First, you pray, and then you practice. God doesn't do it all; you must work God's plan to reach the goal. Your goals will seem more attainable when you break them down into an orderly sequence of events. Don't be too eager to reach your goal. Whenever we try to jump ahead of the Lord, we miss something He has for us, and we may get ourselves into trouble.

Start lining up the resources you'll need to help bring your plans to fulfillment. You need to pray in the people, places, and things that are needed to complete God's plan. Jesus knew He needed resources to establish His church. In Matthew 16:18, Jesus mentioned the church for the first time in His ministry: *"On this rock I will build My church, and the gates of Hades shall not prevail against it."* Jesus had a vision of the completed church. He appointed His disciples to carry out the work and gave them a clear vision of His plans in Acts 1:8: *"You shall be witnesses to Me in Jerusalem, and in all Judea and Samaria, and to the end of the earth."* Then He appointed Paul as an apostle to the gentiles—and the writer of most of the New Testament.

One of the most important things to remember in goal setting is that God is the source of power to achieve the plan. We have things that we must do, but it is the Holy Spirit who enables us to do them. If He doesn't enable us, it is not going to be done the right way. It was the Holy Spirit who enabled the disciples to take the gospel to the ends of the world; they were among the 120 who *"were all filled with the Holy Spirit and began to speak with other tongues, as the Spirit gave them utterance"* (Acts 2:4).

Your number-one key to reaching any goal is the baptism of the Holy Spirit. You need to be saturated with God's Spirit and God's Word. That takes time, and if you make spending time in the Lord's presence your number-one priority, God will see to it that you accomplish more than you ever dreamed you could. You'll accomplish more as a spouse, a mother or father, an employee, and as a grandparent. God will redeem your time and give you the desires of your heart.

Freedom from Failure

"This Book of the Law shall not depart from your
mouth, but you shall meditate in it day and night, . . .
For then you will make your way prosperous,
and then you will have good success."

(JOSHUA 1:8)

God wants His people to succeed, not fail. The Bible confirms over and over that God desires for His children to succeed in every area of life! Let's look at some instances so you can learn how to live the overcoming, successful life promised in the Scriptures.

Many people think they are failures because they don't have any money. But money is *not* the bottom line of success. God can give you creative ideas that result in a flow of money that never stops. Look at Jacob. He fled his home with absolutely nothing and went to work for his deceitful uncle. While there, God gave him unconventional ideas (see Genesis 30–31) to obtain wealth, and when he finally returned home, he was a very successful and wealthy man. Lack of money has never been a problem for God; it needn't be for you either, so stop making an excuse that you don't have any money!

Furthermore, don't ever surrender your God-given dreams to the expressions on people's faces when you tell them, despite how smart they may be. They are not the source of your success—God is. Do you remember when God called Jeremiah to be a prophet? The Lord told him, *"Do not be afraid of their faces, for I am with you to deliver you"* (Jeremiah 1:8). Don't look at people's faces; look at what God told you to do. Besides, God said you succeed by meditating on His Word day and night (see Joshua 1:8). You'll never really succeed by your own intelligence; success will come as you apply the wisdom of God to your situation!

Don't surrender your dreams to your senses; don't limit God to what you've seen or heard can be done through man's puny efforts. What do you think would have happened to Israel if David had given in to his sense of sight when he saw the giant? The Philistines would have overrun the promised land and eliminated the Israelites from our history books. But David said, "God is the one who gave me this idea, and it can be done regardless of what the circumstances look like."

The next excuse for failure is a little tougher: frustration. Maybe you've tried and tried, but nothing ever seems to work out. If you surrender to that frustration, you will never accomplish what God has called you to do. Remember how David responded when Ziklag was burned, and all the women and children were taken captive (see 1 Samuel 30). His men were ready to stone him! Despite his frustration, he faced the disaster by encouraging himself in the Lord (1 Samuel 30:6 KJV). When he did, the Lord spoke to him and told him to pursue the Amalekites. David obeyed, and everything was recovered. David refused to give in to frustration; instead, he encouraged himself in the Lord and turned failure into success. You can too!

Tomorrow, we will look at being in the right frame of mind to pursue your dreams of success. For now, look at some of the excuses you have made over the years, repent, and ask God for a new beginning.

Mind Games

Be renewed in the spirit of your mind.

(EPHESIANS 4:23)

Success is a mind game. If you're not in the right frame of mind, your chances of success are diminished. What you think and believe will play an important role in your success. The devil will do what he can to make your best efforts fail by playing mind games with you.

The devil wants you to live in fear. All of us have attacks of fear. You may be afraid to try because you are afraid to fail. I believe that *not* trying is the biggest failure of all. If God told you to do something, you're better off trying to do it and failing than not trying at all! You will never succeed if you give in to the fear of trying. Successful people overcome the fear of trying.

When you're tired, you can make some wrong decisions. Elijah became exhausted and made the wrong decision. He had just experienced the power of God like never before:

He called down fire on Mt. Carmel, had the prophets of Baal killed, prayed for rain, and then ran 20 miles in the mud from Mt. Carmel to Jezreel (1 Kings 18). But when Jezebel threatened to take his life, he ran off scared; he left the revival that had started on Mt. Carmel. Why? I believe it was because he was physically tired. He wasn't thinking straight, or he wouldn't have feared Jezebel's threat. So, God put him to sleep. You will be up to the Lord's work if you are physically sound and mentally alert; don't sacrifice good judgment to fatigue. Sometimes the most spiritual thing you can do is sleep!

We are living in the "Information Age," and with all this information comes what I call the "frenzies." It's easy to get into a state of panic if we look at all the negative things going on around us.

But, Paul told us not to walk as the gentiles walk *"in the futility of their mind"* (Ephesians 4:17), but to *"be renewed in the spirit of your mind"* (Ephesians 4:23). When Paul was dragged outside the city of Lystra, stoned, and left for dead (see Acts 14), the disciples could have gotten into a frenzy of anguish; instead, they said, "Paul, in Jesus's name, get up!" Their faith brought Paul back to life. Don't surrender to frenzy; surrender to faith!

Our minds won't let us forget the past—past failures, past hurts, past sins. But God has no trouble forgetting those things as long as we have confessed them and forsaken them. The Bible says that *"He will…subdue our iniquities. You will cast all our sins into the depths of the sea"* (Micah 7:19). Your past failures are no excuse for your present inaction because God has put a "No Fishing" sign beside the sea of forgetfulness! What He's forgotten, you need to forget. Don't let past hurts keep you from present joys—don't surrender to past experiences of failure!

I believe that this is the beginning of a whole new wave of success for you. Get out there and do what the Lord has told you to do! Don't let others or the devil lead you down the path to failure. In areas where you have had constant defeat, you are going to see real victory; so rejoice in your newly found freedom.

Tools for Success

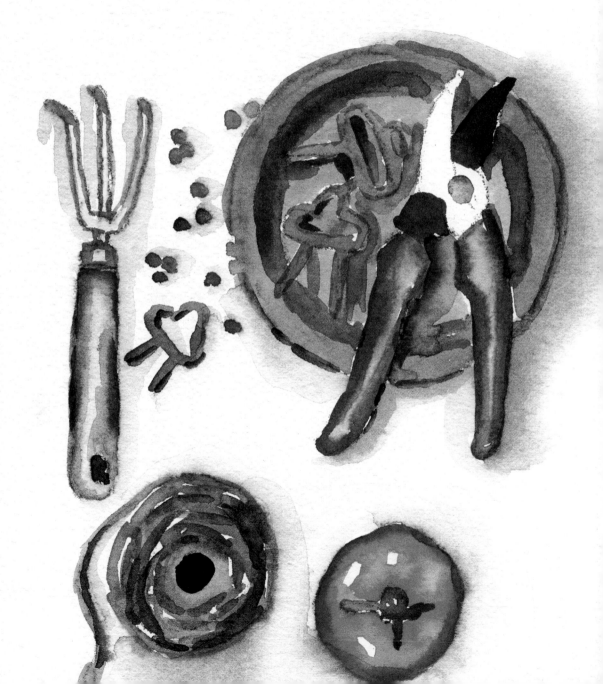

Using Time Wisely

See then that you walk circumspectly, not as fools but
as wise, redeeming the time, because the days are evil.
(EPHESIANS 5:15–16)

*E*veryone has a common ingredient that will enable them to be either totally successful or totally defeated in life. That ingredient is *time,* one of your most valuable resources. God is very concerned that you use it to your best advantage. God puts into our hearts a tremendous desire to achieve and to be productive. Proverbs 13:19 says: *"A desire accomplished is sweet to the soul, but it is an abomination to fools to depart from evil."* If you want the satisfaction of a compliment, then how you use time is important. So, let's look at a few major time traps.

- The Activity Trap: If you aren't sure about God's priorities for you, then you won't accomplish what is most important. Remember Martha? She was so busy, but she failed to accomplish the most important thing because she forgot who the activity was for—Jesus! You can do many things but still miss God's best.

- Procrastination: If you put off the opportunities God gives you, then you often lose out because they are not always available "tomorrow."
- Squandering Time: If you spend too much time watching TV, scrolling online, reading junk, and talking on the phone, then you're probably not achieving much.

God offers Christians promises in His Word that can help us achieve more with our time: *"See then that you walk circumspectly, not as fools but as wise, redeeming the time, because the days are evil"* (Ephesians 5:15–16). According to this scripture, fools waste time, but wise people redeem the time. God's wisdom will show you how to get greater mileage out of each day so that you will be fruitful and productive. Another benefit is "length of days" (see Proverbs 3:13, 16). Notice that "wisdom," "length of days," and "riches and honor" go together.

As Christians, we can stand on these scriptures and see their fruit by applying six practical principles, or keys, to make successful use of our time. When applied to our lives, they can bring forth supernatural results.

1. Put God's Word first every day so you have
   His wisdom for lengthened days.

2. Get up and run with God's plan for your life.
   God sees you as an achiever, and He sees
   you winning our generation to Christ.

3. Set goals; organizing each day determines whether
   you reach long-range goals. Every night, make a list
   of what you plan to accomplish the next day, and
   check off the tasks you have completed; carry the
   unfinished tasks over to the next day. Remember, your
   supernatural God will help you accomplish all of it.

4. Schedule some leeway each day so that
   interruptions won't disrupt your entire schedule.

5. Rely on the Holy Spirit's leading to accomplish God's
   will and accomplish His priorities for your life.

6. Don't waste the precious time God gives you;
   redeem your time, and God will help you make
   the best use of time—your secret for success.

We have to rely on the Holy Spirit's leading to accomplish God's will because emotions are unreliable. Make a commitment to God that you will not waste the precious time He gives you.

Dressed for Success

Therefore take up the whole armor of God, that you may be able to withstand in the evil day, and having done all, to stand. Stand therefore, having girded your waist with truth, having put on the breastplate of righteousness.

(EPHESIANS 6:13–14)

Your heart is a favorite target of the enemy. The devil knows that if he can discourage you, he can steal your blessing, stop your ministry, and spoil your peace. Righteousness protects you from emotional wounds.

When you want to dress for success, you take a shower, fix your hair, and put on your best clothing. As a Christian, you should always dress for spiritual success. Each morning, prepare yourself for victory by putting on the full armor of God. One piece of that armor is your righteousness. Righteousness is the attitude that gives you altitude over every obstacle. As Paul said in Ephesians 6:13–14:

Therefore take up the whole armor of God, that
you may be able to withstand in the evil day,
and having done all, to stand. Stand therefore,
having girded your waist with truth, having
put on the breastplate of righteousness.

Did you notice? Righteousness is like a breastplate that covers your heart. Without the protection of righteousness, your heart can be wounded by the thoughtless or the deliberately negative things people say and do. However, when you surround your emotions with righteousness, the devil's arrows will crash against your armor and bounce harmlessly away. Arrows that target your heart and emotions can't stand up to God's gift of righteousness to born-again Christians and the

promise that *"all things work together for good to those who love God, to those who are the called according to His purpose"* (Romans 8:28).

In addition, righteousness produces power. When you walk in righteousness, you tread in the power and authority of your all-powerful Father God. To others, it may not look like you are in control. In fact, you may not even feel in control. Yet, when you really believe that you are the righteousness of God in Christ, no demon from hell can stand for long between you and your God-given blessing. That means that sickness and disease can be defeated, financial setbacks can't keep you down, and bondages cannot imprison you.

Never forget, tucked into your gift of salvation, you have a powerful, supernatural gift—righteousness! Speak it! Wear it! And walk in the power that makes you rule and reign in this life!

Don't Give Up on Your Dreams

"Please hear this dream which I have dreamed: There we were, binding sheaves in the field. Then behold, my sheaf arose and also stood upright; and indeed your sheaves stood all around and bowed down to my sheaf." And his brothers said to him, "Shall you indeed reign over us? Or shall you indeed have dominion over us?"

(GENESIS 37:6–8)

*D*reams are desires that God plants like seeds in our hearts. Years ago, the Holy Spirit spoke to me and showed me how to make dreams come true, based on the story of Joseph.

Don't give up your dream. At age 17, Joseph had two dreams in which his family bowed down to him. When Joseph told his family these dreams, they were upset with him, and he was pressured to give up his dreams. Criticism from those closest to us is an attack on our dreams. In fact, Joseph's brothers hated him so much that they sold him into slavery!

Don't let anyone steal your dreams. Oftentimes, dreams have to undergo a "death process"—a time when we discover that our efforts are not enough to fulfill our dreams. That's the time to hand your dreams back to God. If He gave them to you, He will resurrect them and bring them to pass.

Practice your dream. Joseph was sold to the wealthy Egyptian, Potiphar. As a slave, Joseph did the only thing he could: he practiced and prepared for the realization of his dreams. Joseph worked hard, God gave him favor, and he was promoted to manager of Potiphar's entire estate. God expects you to prepare and practice for your dream, too.

When Potiphar's wife tried to seduce Joseph, he escaped her advances, but she grabbed his coat as proof of a false accusation of attempted rape. The devil can steal your coat, but he can't steal your dreams. Joseph was incarcerated in Pharaoh's prison. But, God gave Joseph favor, and he became the prison administrator. God didn't remove Joseph from prison; He made it more endurable. Joseph's position gave him opportunity for more—you guessed it—practice and preparation.

Sow into other's dreams. As prison administrator, Joseph oversaw Pharaoah's chief butler and baker. Both men had dreams. Though it looked as though his own dreams wouldn't come to pass, Joseph interpreted their dreams.

God told me to sow into another's dreams at a time when I wanted to realize my own dream of having a radio and TV ministry. It was a bad time financially for me to give, but it was the best time for God because it required faith. I'm here to tell you it worked—but not instantly.

Your day will come. When Joseph was 30 years old, Pharaoh had two unusual dreams that his court magicians couldn't understand. That's when his butler remembered Joseph's ability to interpret dreams. Joseph stood before Pharaoh and interpreted his dreams. When Pharaoh chose Joseph to be the second most powerful man in Egypt, Joseph's dreams finally came true!

If you have given up on your dreams, remember, time cannot steal your dreams unless you let them go. If you have dropped your dreams—pick them up again! And don't forget to sow into others' God-given dreams. My dreams came true for a worldwide ministry, and your dreams can come true, too.

God's Choice for Your Life

Wait, I say, on the LORD!

(PSALM 27:14)

God has given you a very valuable tool called free will that lets you make your own choices. You can choose to follow after God and enjoy the blessings He has for you, or you can choose to do your own thing. Unfortunately, we often find that our choices get us nowhere fast! God's choice is always the best choice for us. He wants the very best for you, and He knows just how to get it to you, though it often takes waiting: *"Wait, I say, on the LORD!"* (Psalm 27:14).

Scripture gives us examples of people who chose one life only to have their plans totally changed by God. Paul wanted to take the gospel to Asia, but the Holy Spirit stopped him (see Acts 16:6–8). Paul was sure that Asia was God's will for him, but he left himself open to the direction and guidance of the Holy Spirit. When he got to Troas, God closed the door to Paul's first choice, but opened another door. He had a vision in which a man pleaded with him to come to Macedonia, and he concluded *"that the Lord had called us to preach the gospel to them"* (Acts 16:10).

Paul knew that God must have had a good reason for direct-ing him to Greece. He had learned to accept God's choices for his life. So, Paul went to Philippi. Near a riverbank, he met a group of women gathered for a prayer service. One of those women was Lydia, who became the first convert in Europe and was no doubt instrumental in spreading the gospel throughout that region; we know there was a thriving church in Philippi when Paul was in Rome. Because of Paul's second choice, many of us with European ancestry have "inherited" Christianity from those seeds planted nearly 2,000 years ago.

Peter also learned a lesson about second choices after Jesus's resurrection. Even though Peter had spent years with Jesus, he appeared to turn his back on God's will for his life by

returning to the fishing trade. John 21 tells us Peter and several of the disciples fished all night but caught nothing. That's because it wasn't God's will for Peter to be a fisherman. God had chosen Peter to help spread the gospel throughout the world. So even though they had toiled all night long, they weren't successful. At daybreak, a man was waiting for them on the shore. When He directed them to throw the nets out on the other side of the boat, they caught so many fish that they had trouble bringing the fish in. When Peter finally realized that the man was Jesus, he swam to shore.

Jesus then reaffirmed to Peter what God's choice was for his life: *"Feed my sheep"* (John 21:17). Peter, the man who didn't want to fool around with the gospel and who had denied Jesus three times, was now told that Jesus still wanted him as a leader in His church. When Peter made God's choice his choice, he found great joy as well as success.

Finally, let's look at Jesus: *"He came to His own, and His own did not receive Him"* (John 1:11). Jesus's first choice was to save the Jews. We were His second choice, but when the gospel was preached among the gentiles, it spread to the world. Eventually, the Jews—Jesus's first choice—will call Him their Savior, too.

There may be many times when you think you are a failure because your first choice didn't work out the way you planned. But if you wait on God and earnestly desire His choice for your life, He will meet you where you are and lead you into the place He has prepared for you.

No Compromise

*"Our God whom we serve is able to deliver
us from the burning fiery furnace, and He
will deliver us from your hand, O king."*

(DANIEL 3:17)

When you purpose in your heart to accomplish God's will, He will give you divine favor. When you "purpose" to do something, you set it as an aim, intention, or goal for yourself. The Old Testament gives us a marvelous example of four young men who did exactly this. Though taken as slaves to Babylon, they had been raised to serve God with all their hearts. In Babylon, they were superbly educated and dedicated to the king's service. Their Hebrew names were changed to Shadrach, Meshach, Abednego, and Belteshazzar—names that reflected the idolatrous nature of their new home. These young Hebrews seemed to be in the darkest situation of their lives. But light always overcomes darkness. They never compromised their faith. If you purpose in your heart like these boys did (see Daniel 1:8), then you won't be changed by dark circumstances; instead, you will change them!

The key to changing your circumstances is to purpose in your heart to be like God and to begin acting on that purpose in faith—in other words, no compromise. Once they declared their intentions, God did something very special; God not only gave these young men favor, He gave them knowledge and wisdom. They had an ability to understand dreams and were 10 times wiser than anyone else (see Daniel 1:20). Likewise, when you purpose in your heart to take the stand that these young men did, God will give you favor—divine favor—and the wisdom to change your circumstances.

When they took a stand for God, these four young men received positions that the Babylonians would have loved to have held! God turned these slaves into leaders. I won't pretend that it's easy to live uncompromisingly, and I won't say it's easy to take a stand for God. The devil will try to push you out of that stand like he did with these young men.

In Daniel 3, Nebuchadnezzar set up an idol and commanded all his leaders to bow down to it. If they refused, they would be thrown into a fiery furnace.

That took care of the rebels—except for these young men who refused to bow down. Daniel 3:17 tells us that when these three young men were faced with this life-or-death decision, they announced, *"Our God whom we serve is able to deliver us from the burning fiery furnace, and He will deliver us from your hand, O king."* Nebuchadnezzar was so angry at their rebellion that he had the fiery furnace heated seven times more than it was usually heated before throwing them in. Their response was to trust God to deliver them from the furnace and from the king's hand as well. That's faith! That's taking a stand!

There are two ways God can deliver you from fiery trials: He can either deliver you *from* them or *out* of them. You're going to have to purpose that you will never compromise. In this instance, God didn't deliver the Hebrews *from* the fire. They were bound and thrown in, but then God stepped in with them. Nebuchadnezzar's eyes must have bugged out when he saw four men in there! He even exclaimed that the fourth man looked like the Son of God!

No matter how fiery your trial, someone else is with you—Jesus! God can put you in a position where fire won't burn you, and you won't even smell like smoke. He will go with you if you purpose in your heart to act on His Word. Purpose in your heart to do things God's way. You can change circumstances, people, and maybe even kingdoms!

Righting Wrongs

"And he shall make restitution for the harm that he has done in regard to the holy thing, and shall add one-fifth to it and give it to the priest. So the priest shall make atonement for him with the ram of the trespass offering, and it shall be forgiven him."

(LEVITICUS 5:16)

*H*as there ever been a time when someone hurt you—or really "did you wrong"? Maybe your spouse or children took advantage of you. Perhaps there was a time when you didn't get a raise or a position you thought was well deserved. Or maybe someone stole from you or gossiped against you, causing you to murmur, "That does it! I'm going to get even if it's the last thing I do!"

How do you right a wrong? God has a way of turning life's disadvantages into advantages. If you follow what I call the "doctrine of the fifth," you will end up with more than you lost in life's unfair situations.

Under Old Testament law, if an Israelite wronged someone, he was required to offer a sacrifice to restore his fellowship with God. To the value of the sacrifice, such as a $100 lamb, 20 percent or $20, was calculated and then given to the priest. If the Israelite stole someone's property, he was required to return the item to the rightful owner plus 20 percent, or one-fifth, of its value.

This doctrine of the fifth is easy to remember because it's found in Leviticus 5:16:

"And he shall make restitution for the harm that he has done in regard to the holy thing, and shall add one-fifth to it and give it to the priest. So the priest shall make atonement for him with the ram of the trespass offering, and it shall be forgiven him."

Numbers 5:7 adds: *"Then he shall confess the sin which he has committed. He shall make restitution for his trespass in full, plus one-fifth of it, and give it to the one he has wronged."*

Using the doctrine of the fifth, God turned a disadvantage into an advantage; the priest was happy with the extra one-fifth, and the victim received what was stolen plus 20 percent of its value. But what about the person who committed the offense? His sins were forgiven, he was reconciled to his brother, and, of course, he was motivated to be honest for the rest of his life.

Consider this matter of the fifth from a little different perspective. What if *you* are the one who has been wronged? What if someone stole from you, denied your raise at work, or damaged your reputation? That is when you need to put this principle of the fifth into operation and allow God to pay you back *20% more* than you lost. Let God right your wrong. Extend grace—don't take revenge!

Finding God's Glory in the Tough Places of Your Life

"Prepare the way of the LORD; make straight in the desert a highway for our God. Every valley shall be exalted and every mountain and hill brought low; the crooked places shall be made straight and the rough places smooth; the glory of the LORD shall be revealed, and all flesh shall see it together; for the mouth of the LORD has spoken."

(ISAIAH 40:3–5)

God wants to reveal His glory in your toughest situation and to flood the dry places of your life, but He can't come into your wilderness until you prepare a way for Him. In this passage, Isaiah tells us to prepare a highway for Him, and he mentions four hindrances to doing that.

Isaiah says that every valley needs to be exalted. There may be a valley between God and you. Sometimes this valley is low self-esteem; you let your opinion of yourself blot out what God says about you. Gideon (Judges 6) was a man of low self-esteem. When the angel of the Lord called him a "mighty man of valor," he responded, "Who me? I'm powerless." Gideon's estimation of himself needed to come up to what God said about him. God wanted to reveal His glory through a victory over the Midianites, but Gideon's low self-esteem was blocking the completion of God's highway. How about you? Begin to look at yourself through God's eyes and believe God's Word. You can confess: "I can do all things through Christ who strengthens me," (Philippians 4:13) and "we have the mind of Christ" (1 Corinthians 2:16).

Maybe the obstacle blocking that highway is not a valley but a mountain—like a mountain of pride. The opposite of low self-esteem is pride—thinking more of ourselves than what God says about us. Nebuchadnezzar had a mountain of pride that God had to deal with before His glory could be revealed. He thought that he'd built his empire without God's help. His pride was leveled when he lost his mind and lived outdoors like an animal for seven years! When he humbled himself and acknowledged God's goodness and grace in his life, he came back to his senses. Don't allow pride to come between you and the glory of the Lord!

The other kind of mountain is strictly devil-devised. You need to speak to it in order to see it removed: *"I say to you, if you have faith as a mustard seed, you will say to this mountain, 'Move from here to there,'*

and it will move" (Matthew 17:20). Devil-devised problems, whether financial, physical, or personal, can be destroyed through words of faith.

Next, Isaiah said that the crooked and rough places would be made straight and smoothed out. Frankly, are you crooked in some area of your life? God cannot bless where there is something crooked. Sometimes it's little things—coming to work late, cursing, or criticizing others. Maybe you have some rough places, like a nasty disposition or difficulty getting along with others. Look at the disciple John. Once, John wanted Jesus to strike some people with lightning, but today John is known as "the apostle of love." What happened? Jesus smoothed out his rough places. He was flooded with God's love when he allowed Jesus to reveal a highway for God's glory.

God can help you prepare a highway for God's glory to be revealed in your life. It starts with repentance. Pray with me:

> Dear Lord, I repent of those wrong attitudes that
> have kept me from seeing myself as you see me. I
> renounce any pride that hinders you from moving
> in my circumstances, and I confess and forsake
> the crooked areas of my life. Lord Jesus, smooth
> out the rough areas of my personality and flood
> me with your love and life. In Jesus's name, amen!

Experiencing the Glory of God

*And the Angel of God, who went before the camp of
Israel, moved and went behind them; and the pillar of
cloud went from before them and stood behind them.
So it came between the camp of the Egyptians and the
camp of Israel. Thus it was a cloud and darkness to the
one, and it gave light by night to the other, so that the one
did not come near the other all that night. Then Moses
stretched out his hand over the sea; and the LORD caused
the sea to go back . . . and the waters were divided.*

(EXODUS 14:19–21)

Just as the Holy Spirit is a person and not a thing, the
glory of God is not a feeling, goose bumps, or a once-
in-a-lifetime occurrence. Simply put, the glory of God is the
manifestation of the presence, the person, and the power of
God. If you have ever experienced or seen God's glory, you will
never be the same. Nothing on this earth can compare to this
powerful manifestation of God's presence.

God's glory is often manifested in the form of a cloud. The
Israelites were intimately acquainted with this manifestation,
more so than New Testament believers. It was a pillar of cloud

by day and a pillar of fire by night. In Exodus 14, God's glory protected the Israelites and confused the enemy. In this crisis, Pharaoh's army was behind them, and the Red Sea loomed ahead. As the Israelites began to murmur, God's glory—the manifestation of the presence, the person, and the power of God—moved on their behalf, and the Red Sea parted. The glory cloud watched over and protected the Israelites from certain death and delivered them from destruction. God's glory serves the same purpose in the lives of believers today.

Once the tabernacle was set up, the cloud lingered there: *"Whenever the cloud was taken up from above the tabernacle, . . . the children of Israel would journey; and in the place where the cloud settled, there the children of Israel would pitch their tents"* (Numbers 9:17). They followed God's leading; He communicated with them, and they learned to look to Him for instruction. It's important to follow God's leading; if you follow others, you could end up in a self-imposed wilderness. But if you follow God's glorious leading, the result will be victory because He will not lead you astray.

Unlike the Israelites, New Testament believers have the indwelling of the Holy Spirit, who leads us into all truth. If you don't think you are hearing from God, you may be in a wilderness and need to experience God's glory. It is in the glory of His presence that He speaks to us and performs the impossible.

God wants you and the entire body of Christ to experience His glory. In Acts 1, Jesus was "caught up" to heaven in God's glory. When He returns, He will come back in a cloud, and we will be caught up together with Him into the glory of God. The glory of God is not a new move of God. It is simply another facet of our heavenly Father and a vehicle for Him to lead, guide, and minister to His people. It is not a Pentecostal or charismatic "thing." The glory of God is a "God thing," and it is gaining momentum throughout the land.

Change Transcends Time

*But we all, with unveiled face, beholding as in a mirror
the glory of the Lord, are being transformed into the same
image from glory to glory, just as by the Spirit of the Lord.*

(2 CORINTHIANS 3:18)

God wants you to change to become like Jesus. The more
you get in line with the Word, the more you are going to be
like Him because His Word is His essence, His being, His stan-
dard, and His desire. The more you get into His Word, the more
He changes your soul. You begin to think as He thinks and see
as He sees. There is no other way to change except to go to the
changeless one and let Him change you.

It isn't what you do to the outside of yourself that changes
you. The key to making a permanent change is found in
2 Corinthians 3:18: *"But we all, with unveiled face, beholding as
in a mirror the glory of the Lord, are being transformed into the
same image from glory to glory, just as by the Spirit of the Lord."*
As you behold Him, His glory begins to change you. When you
truly behold Him for the first time, God changes you—spirit,

soul, and body. He gives you a new nature. Why? Because your old one won't change. However, your new nature will love God wholeheartedly and will change your life.

When Jesus was raised from the grave, He received a glorified body. If we are like Jesus, then we, too, can expect the same. God is going to give you a new body. Even Job foresaw this change: *"If a man die, shall he live again? All the days of my hard service I will wait, till my change comes"* (Job 14:14). Change is a key to eternal life!

This simple acrostic will help you remember how change occurs:

C. **Challenge.** Heart-felt changes are not impossible or difficult. The challenge is to let go and let God.

H. **Heart.** The change begins in your heart. It won't begin on the outside the way the world thinks, but in your heart, where God can change you from the inside out.

A. **Attitude.** Your attitude will change once your heart is changed and will reflect the continuing change in your heart.

N. **Notice.** When you notice Jesus, behold Him, and spend time in His presence, you can go from glory to glory through the change wrought in you.

G. **Goal.** Your number-one goal is to be like Jesus, conformed to His image.

E . **Expectancy.** You can expect to change when you behold Him. Your heart will change. Your attitude will change. Your circumstances will change. And your body will one day change because you are going to spend eternity with God. Our expectancy is not just for this life. Our expectancy is to behold His face for this life and for all eternity.

God will change your spirit by giving you a new nature. He will change your soul as you become more involved in the Word of God and spend time in prayer. When you follow after Jesus and behold His face, you choose to walk with God for all eternity. When it comes time for us to meet the Lord face-to-face, *"We shall all be changed—in a moment, in the twinkling of an eye, at the last trumpet. For the trumpet will sound, and the dead will be raised incorruptible, and we shall be changed"* (1 Corinthians 15:51–53). Blink your eyes! That's how fast you're going to change!

Stress Buster

*Trust in the LORD with all your heart, and lean
not on your own understanding; in all your ways
acknowledge Him, and He shall direct your paths.*

(PROVERBS 3:5–6)

Life is lived in the fast lane—road rage, emails, texts, cell phones, deadlines, and all of the *pressure* that goes with it! Technological advances have simplified some things and complicated others. Relaxing dinners in a quiet restaurant are long gone. Cell phones interrupt conversation and digestion. Stress and our ways of handling pressure haven't changed much over the years. When stress levels take us to the edge, we tend to manage in one of two ways: fight or flight.

Stress was common in Bible times. Jacob faced stress when his brother, Esau, threatened to kill him; Job was overwhelmed when he lost all he had except a nagging wife; Elijah went from spiritual heights to the pit of fear after wicked Jezebel

threatened to kill him. How did these men respond? Jacob and Job opted to fight—Jacob wrestled with the Lord (Genesis 32:24), and Job argued with God and his accusers. Elijah chose flight: he fled in fear (1 Kings 19:3).

Neither fight nor flight deals with the real issue—they take us around the mountain instead of over it. Without a fundamental change in approach, the problem of stress will continue to crop up, and we'll go around the same mountain again and again.

How do you deal with the stress in your life? Are you in survival mode? Do you squeak through with coping mechanisms while bracing for the next crisis? If stress is showing up in arguments at the dinner table or highway shouting matches at 65 m.p.h., if you're compulsively cleaning the house or camping out on the couch binge-watching entire seasons of TV shows at a time, it's time for a change.

King Jehoshaphat found the key to finding relief—God. Surrounded by a hostile army, he was at the end of his rope. Fighting was not an option, and neither was escape, so he was forced to look upward for his answer: *"For we have no power against this great multitude that is coming against us; nor do we know what to do, but our eyes are upon You"* (2 Chronicles 20:12).

Like Jehoshaphat, we are not limited to the world's techniques. When stress comes knocking, turn to God. Use His Word and take authority over the stress that can zap your strength and diminish your life. Proverbs 3:5–6 tells us the right response and its outcome: *"Trust in the LORD with all your heart, and lean not on your own understanding; in all your ways acknowledge Him, and He shall direct your paths."*

Regardless of how bad circumstances look, you can offset the pressure by drawing closer to God. He never expected us to bear the brunt of stress but gave us a solution for it: *"Do not be anxious about anything, but in every situation, . . . present your requests to God. And the peace of God, which transcends all understanding, will guard your hearts and your minds in Christ Jesus"* (Philippians 4:6–7 NIV). I'm so thankful that God doesn't give us complicated formulas that add to our stress; He simply and gently reminds us to turn our eyes to Him. As our gaze becomes fixed on "The Answer," our battle becomes His, and His victory becomes ours. The results will astound you!

Overcoming
Struggle

Pressure? Press into God

My soul follows close behind You;
Your right hand upholds me.

(PSALM 63:8)

We all have some kind of pressure in our lives—whether it be finances, children, spouse, or illness. How you deal with pressure determines whether you wind up a winner or wallow in failure. Look at the Syrophoenician woman—a Greek with no covenant rights, no relationship with God, a woman under pressure and with no hope. Despite being rebuked by Jesus, she refused to allow humiliation to keep her from receiving her daughter's life back. No matter how she was pressured, she pressed into Jesus and received her answer (see Mark 7:24–30). She was a winner!

When you are under pressure, you have a choice—you can press into God and find relief, or press into others and make matters worse. Psalm 63:8 shows that David learned that God would meet him when he was pressured, *"My soul follows close behind You; Your right hand upholds me."*

At certain key moments in his life, Jacob was a man under pressure. Those times illustrate ways we can press into God for our victory. Jacob was called a deceiver. He purchased the birthright from his hungry brother, Esau, with a bowl of stew. Then he deceived his father, Isaac, to steal the blessing of the firstborn from Esau.

His life threatened by Esau, Jacob fled (see Genesis 27–28). That first night as a fugitive, Jacob must have been fearful and anxious, for, in a dream, God reassured Jacob and promised He would be with him. If you press into God when you are under pressure, He will speak to you, too, be it through a vision, scripture, person; somehow, someway God will reassure you about your future like He did Jacob.

Laban, Jacob's father-in-law, stole years of service from Jacob and repeatedly reduced his promised wages. So, God taught Jacob how to prosper (see Genesis 30), showing him how to handle his flock so it would produce speckled, spotted, and striped offspring because those were to be his wages. God will do the same for you. You may be under financial pressure. Your wages may seem to just disappear, coming in one way and going out 50 ways. When you press into God, He will teach you how to prosper, and even provide a miracle to meet your needs, *"Thus says the* L*ORD, your Redeemer, the Holy One of Israel: 'I am the Lord your God, who teaches you to profit, who leads you by the way you should go'"* (Isaiah 48:17).

When he was returning home, Jacob knew he would have to face Esau. But Jacob had finally learned how to deal with pressure—where to apply it and where not to apply it. Jacob didn't blame Esau or his mother for having to flee home. Rather, Jacob pressed into God. Genesis 32 tells us that the night before meeting his brother, Jacob wrestled with an angel and said, *"I will not let you go unless You bless me!"* (v. 26). The result was that Jacob, the deceiver, got a new name, "Israel," which means "he will rule as God," and "God prevails"; and he became the father of the 12 tribes of Israel.

When the enemy tries to put the pressure on you, remember that Jesus was under great pressure at Gethsemane, agonizing over the pain and shame to come. As He pressed into God, He was able to go to the cross, beat up the devil and his demons, and leap out of the grave in total victory. You can do the same. Put the pressure back on the devil by reminding him that, in Christ, you are a new creation. When you're under pressure, press into God, grab hold of His Word, and don't let go until it changes you. Then rejoice in your victory!

When God Doesn't Make Sense

I count everything as loss compared to the possession of the priceless privilege... of knowing Christ Jesus my Lord.

(PHILIPPIANS 3:8 AMP)

In the midst of a crisis, have you ever thought, "God, where are you?" In difficult times, there's so much we don't know. That's when we must stick with what we *do* know. When we don't understand, God is still faithful. When life seems unfair, God is still just. When you can't make sense of anything else, He will never leave you. He is right there with you, even in the midst of your pain, questions, and confusion.

One thing I know for sure is that God has a purpose. Romans 8:28 can turn your doubt and despair into hope and peace of mind: *"All things work together for good to those who love God, to those who are the called according to His purpose."*

When we think of suffering and loss, the first person that comes to mind is Job. He faced every imaginable tragedy: the loss of his children, material and financial ruin, and

excruciating, physical pain. Yet, sitting among the ashes of his life, Job declared, *"Though He slay me, yet will I trust Him"* (Job 13:15). His absolute trust in God became the platform upon which God rebuilt, restored, and resurrected Job's life!

God took his devastation and used it for a greater purpose—and He can do the same for you. Perhaps you find yourself in a situation that makes no sense. Your heart's cry may be, "How can I trust God when the world seems to be crumbling beneath my feet?" I want to offer some simple steps to help you find your footing when life has knocked you off your feet.

Continue to obey God even when you don't understand your circumstances. Keep doing what He's given you to do. Don't turn your back on those things that bring you joy. If you

are ministering to others, stick with it. Keep reading your Bible, even when it seems as if reading doesn't do any good. Trust God beyond what you see. Trust the nature of God more than your own understanding. Refuse to believe that your life is over or that nothing good can come from your trouble. Trusting God is based on His everlasting love for you—never on what is going on around you. Make Romans 8:38–39 your theme: *"For I am persuaded that* [nothing] *. . . shall be able to separate* [me] *from the love of God which is in Christ Jesus* [my] *Lord."*

Recognize these moments as opportunities to know God more intimately. There is such sweet fellowship when you come to God broken, even desperate. Intimacy is forged when we reveal our deepest disappointments and broken dreams. Then, like Paul, we can cry out, *"I count everything as loss compared to the possession of the priceless privilege . . . of knowing Christ Jesus my Lord and of progressively becoming more deeply and intimately acquainted with Him"* (Philippians 3:8 AMPC).

When you want to give up because life doesn't make sense; when you're tempted to doubt God's love for you; when you just don't understand, remember Jesus, *"Who for the joy that was set before Him endured the cross"* (Hebrews 12:2). The joy before Him was you and me.

Beauty for Ashes

"[The Lord will] give [you] beauty for ashes, the oil of joy for mourning, the garment of praise for the spirit of heaviness; that [you] may be called trees of righteousness, the planting of the LORD, that He may be glorified."

(ISAIAH 61:3)

Everyone has "ashes" in their lives—the parts of your life that have been damaged by loss or the actions of others. We all have experienced things that have hurt us—wounds that have never healed. Yet, you don't have to live with your ashes any longer. You can be free!

Isaiah 61:3 promises that the Lord will *"give [you] beauty for ashes, the oil of joy for mourning, the garment of praise for the spirit of heaviness; that [you] may be called trees of righteousness, the planting of the LORD, that He may be glorified."* God can touch and heal the wounded and broken places in your heart and make beauty arise from the ashes of your past. Exchanging ashes for beauty has a lot to do with your mind. You can trade your depression and awful memories of hurt, pain, and abuse for God's beautiful outlook.

Some people have lived in their ashes for so long that their pain has permeated every part of their lives. They are frozen in the past and live out of its painful memories. According to Isaiah 44:20, *"He feeds on ashes; a deceived heart has turned him aside."* All they can do is talk about ancient wounds and tragedy. You can spend your life talking about how you've been mistreated, how your husband left you, how your wife was unfaithful, or how your boss sabotaged your career. You can waste your life "eating" ashes. If you never give them up, you will never receive the beauty God has for you. But, when you take your ashes to Jesus, He cleanses and saturates you with the sweet fragrance of joy.

Job was a man who knew grief. He lost everything all at once—his 10 children, his health, his wealth; he even lost the support of his wife. When Job—in the midst of ruin—sat scratching himself with a potsherd, he must have thought things couldn't get worse; then, his "friends" showed up to torment him. Yet, there was beauty for ashes in Job's future. When Job gave his ashes to God, he received 10 new children, twice the wealth he lost, and long life.

A pastor from Central America shared his "ashes" story with me. He'd married a beautiful, Spirit-filled woman. He pastored a large church, and things were going well until his wife left him and their young son for a lesbian lover. The divorce cost him his pastoral credentials, his church, and former friends. Seemingly, he was totally defeated. His life in shambles, he gave his ashes to God, and things began to change. He was accepted into another denomination, and his ministry began to flourish. Then God gave him a second wife and a beautiful daughter. Today, he has a very large church, and his son from his first wife is also a successful pastor. But the story doesn't end there. The godly mother of his former wife didn't give up on her lesbian daughter. After 10 years of prayer, her daughter came back to God, and she has a ministry, too.

Both these men gave their ashes of brokenness and hurt to God, and He gave them a greater victory than they could imagine. You can do the same! When you get rid of your ashes by giving God your past hurts, you become a tree that produces good fruit. You will be fresh and flourishing—a person who can have a good, happy, and fulfilling life. God will crown you with beauty, pour the healing oil of joy on your wounds, and dress you in a magnificent robe of praise.

Turning Opposition into Opportunity

[Jesus] went about doing good and healing all who were oppressed by the devil, for God was with Him.

(ACTS 10:38)

D id you know that God sees opposition as an opportunity? Contention, hatred, oppression, and strife can stop you in your tracks; or they can make you see the opportunity God has for you. God wants you to take advantage of every opportunity to win in every situation. Everyone has a choice: we can turn our oppression into an opportunity, or we can let the oppression triumph over us.

Oppression and opposition have two sources, the devil and men. All of us are guilty of being oppressors. It's a very real human trait, one which God's Word explicitly warns against: *"Do not oppress the widow or*

the fatherless, the alien or the poor. Let none of you plan evil in his heart against his brother" (Zechariah 7:10). Exodus 22:21 says, "You shall neither mistreat a stranger nor oppress him." Proverbs 14:31 tells us not to oppress the poor, and Leviticus 25:14 says we are not to oppress one another. God also warns us not to use oppression to manipulate people: "Do not trust in oppression" because God "render[s] to each one according to his work" (Psalm 62:10, 12).

The second source of opposition and oppression is the devil. God has promised to deliver you from Satan's devious acts. Jesus spent a lot of time on Earth delivering people from the devil's attacks, and He is still doing the same today: "[Jesus] went about doing good and healing all who were oppressed by the devil, for God was with Him" (Acts 10:38). He will anoint you and nourish you even in the presence of the devil! David knew well what it was like to be oppressed from every angle and learned to turn it into opportunity: "You prepare a table before me in the presence of my enemies; You anoint my head with oil; my cup runs over" (Psalm 23:5).

Genesis 26 shows us that Isaac met opposition and turned it into an opportunity. Because of a famine, Isaac went to Gerar, where God so prospered him that King Abimelech finally asked him to leave. So, Isaac went to the Valley of Gerar, where the Philistines who inhabited the land came against him. They had stopped up all the wells that Abraham had dug. When Isaac re-dug one well, the Philistines claimed the water for themselves. Isaac called that well "Esek," which means "contention" or "strife." Now, Isaac had a choice to make. He could have become involved in a real battle over the water rights, but instead, he dug another well. Once more, he met with strife, so he called the well *"Sitnah"* which means "strife."

Yet, he didn't react; rather, he acted God's way and got results. Genesis 26:22 tells us that he moved away, dug another well, and became fruitful: *"For now the LORD has made room for us, and we shall be fruitful in the land."* Once he decided to turn opposition into opportunity, the Lord appeared to him and said, *"I am the God of your father Abraham; do not fear, for I am with you. I will bless you and multiply your descendants for My servant Abraham's sake"* (Genesis 26:24). It goes on to say that Isaac finally settled down, and God kept prospering him.

God's opportunity always leads to victory. Remember, opposition and opportunity will lead you in two totally different directions. If you see opposition as God's opportunity, it can lead you to victory. If something is wrong, focus on the opportunity of what God can do and how you can pray it through. Remember, we're not here to oppress each other; we're here to bless each other!

Overcoming Strife

*With humility of mind regard one another
as more important than yourselves.*

(PHILIPPIANS 2:3 NASB)

I f you have ever tried to resolve a conflict without God's help, you know how frustrating it can be. So, I looked for a godly, simple way to win a fight—a win-win solution that anyone can apply in their life. I don't need a complicated formula. I need a simple strategy to diffuse the situation. I believe the following will help you overcome strife, God's way.

First, identify why you're fighting so you don't blow things out of proportion. We often find ourselves in the middle of conflict and don't know how we got there. Sometimes it's because of conflicting viewpoints or different values; maybe it's just because we're tired. If you can discover why you're fighting and why the other person is fighting, it'll help you resolve the issues. It's also important to ask yourself if the conflict is important enough to risk the relationship.

Second, because it's a contributing factor to conflict, get rid of pride. Consider James 4:1–3 (NIV): *"What causes fights and quarrels among you?... You desire but do not have,... you quarrel and fight. You do not have because you do not ask God. When you ask, you do not receive, because you ask with wrong motives."* When we argue because we want our own way, strife enters. The fact that the middle letter of the word pride is "I" demonstrates how thinking that the world revolves around us causes conflict. Remembering that sin thrives in an environment of pride, but love thrives in an atmosphere of humility, can help us take a big step toward pushing strife out of our lives.

Third, there is no more effective strategy in dealing with conflict than to take the low road, so embrace humility. James 4:6 says: *"God resists the proud, but gives grace to the humble."* This approach says, "I could be wrong. You may be right." When you move from trying to be right to trying to understand and keep the peace, you'll see that this attitude totally defuses pride. The key to embracing humility is found in Philippians 2:3–4 (NASB): *"Do nothing from selfishness or empty conceit, but with humility of mind regard one another as more important than yourselves; do not merely look out for your own personal interests, but also for the interests of others."*

Finally, fight fair. Have you ever said something in the heat of an argument and wished you could take it back?

I think we all have, and that's why it's important to "fight fair." If you're arguing, don't purposely bring up the other person's weak spots or "hot buttons." If you start tearing them down and bringing up issues that have nothing to do with the argument—that's not fighting fair. You're deviating from the issues and adding fuel to the fire. James 4:11 (NLT) says, *"Don't speak evil against each other."*

If you're going to disagree, then work toward a common goal, outcome, and resolution. Go for a win-win. Help the person you're in conflict with to win, and you'll win as well. Don't have the attitude of "I'm going to win this one—no matter what it takes." If you'll remember these four simple steps and ask the Holy Spirit to help you, you can overcome strife God's way. His strategy restores the peace and creates a win-win situation every time.

Lifelines

*"Behold! The Lamb of God who takes
away the sin of the world!"*

(JOHN 1:29)

Let's face it—even Christians encounter challenges.
The Bible clearly says: *"Do not think it strange concerning
the fiery trial which is to try you, as though some strange thing
happened to you"* (1 Peter 4:12).

A while back, a man on the verge of suicide called our
prayer center. He was in despair: his wife had left him, he
had lost his job, and he had little food left. Our prayer warrior
prayed with him. Together, they bound Satan's attacks and
spoke God's Word into the situation. The change in the caller
was immediately evident; his voice changed, and he became
more optimistic. When it looked as if all hope was gone, it was
prayer and the Word of God that strengthened him and prepared him to persevere.

During a crisis, we can easily overlook the key links along
God's lifeline to triumph. A crisis is God's opportunity to bring
you a miracle. Yet, to have total victory, we must use every link

He gives us. The four "Lifeline Links" below will help you handle the pressure and stay on the path to victory regardless of any challenge.

Lifeline Link #1: Look to the Lamb. When in crisis mode, we either can look to the Lord, or we can quit. Enslaved in Egypt, the Israelites were terribly oppressed, seemingly with no way out. Yet, Moses looked to God. God told Moses to have each family kill a lamb—the symbol of Christ—and sprinkle its blood on their doorposts. They obeyed. That very night, they were delivered. Their crisis had become an opportunity for a miracle.

Lifeline Link #2: If you've missed it—repent. Remember—crises can come even when you're doing God's will. Being in the wilderness doesn't always mean you have disobeyed God. Satan will try to convince you otherwise. Resist him, and if you

have caused the crisis, admit it. Confess your sin, and allow Jesus, the Lamb, to forgive you. *"If we confess our sins, He is faithful and just to forgive us our sins and to cleanse us from all unrighteousness"* (1 John 1:9).

Lifeline Link #3: Pray a prayer of agreement. If you're in a trial, invite the Lamb into the situation. Ask another Christian to pray in agreement with you. Proclaim His Lordship over all that concerns you and ask for His guidance to overcome the enemy. Matthew 18:19 says: *"Again I say to you that if two of you agree on earth concerning anything that they ask, it will be done for them by My Father in heaven."*

Lifeline Link #4: Rejoice in God's provision. Because Jesus was your sacrificial Lamb and died on the cross for you, you can bring Him into each of life's bitter experiences. When John the Baptist saw Jesus, he cried out, *"Behold! The Lamb of God who takes away the sin of the world!"* (John 1:29). John recognized Jesus as the one who would rescue mankind from the crises and trials of a fallen world.

Whatever crisis you are facing, turn to the Lamb and catch hold of the lifeline He offers you. Rejoice that God has provided the Lamb to turn the bitter herbs of life's trials into the sweet cup of deliverance!

No Way Out? Think Again!

God is faithful, who will not allow you to be
tempted beyond what you are able, but with
the temptation will also make the way of
escape, that you may be able to bear it.

(1 CORINTHIANS 10:13)

*D*o you need a way out of temptation? I have good news for you—God has a way out designed specifically for you! First Corinthians 10:13 says three things about the temptations that may come your way: *"No temptation has overtaken you except such as is common to man; but God is faithful, who will not allow you to be tempted beyond what you are able, but with the temptation will also make the way of escape, that you may be able to bear it."* First, it says that temptations are "common." Temptations, though they may come in different forms, happen to everyone. Second, the faithfulness of God will cause you to prevail in every situation. Third, God will provide a way out of the situation so that you will be able to successfully endure it.

Adversity and temptation come to steal the Word of God out of your heart so that it will not bear fruit in your life. The devil would love to get you on a detour so that you miss what God has for you. He will try all kinds of things to rob you of God's plan for your life. We all have people and circumstances that could get us off target with God and cause us to detour from His chosen path. But God promises that when you are faced with a temptation, He will either help you through it or take you out of it. God will give you a way out! Many believers think they will escape adversity and temptation by the "skin of their teeth." However, as Christians, you should not think of just barely getting by. I want you to think *triumph*. I want you to think *victory* because that is what the Word of God says.

There are two ways to escape adversity—God's way and man's way. The most common form of escape in today's pleasure-oriented society is through entertainment. Christians and non-Christians alike spend countless hours of their lives watching TV, scrolling online, or some other form of entertainment. By bombarding their minds with make-believe, they think they can escape their problems and pretend they don't exist. The world's system says, "Don't think! Let us amuse you. Take your mind off your problems and watch TV!"

But Isaiah 1:18 says, "'*Come now, and let us reason together,*' *says the L*ORD." God wants to speak to you and do something very supernatural in the time of your temptation. You don't have to yield to a man-made or self-made detour.

If ever a man needed a way of escape, it was Job. Not only had he lost his wealth, health, and children, but he also had bad breath (see Job 19:17 NIV). His friends accused him of having sin in his life, and because of that sin, they said God had judged him. However, in the midst of his temptation, Job had a revelation of God like he had never had before. Out of that revelation came a double portion of blessings—God doubled everything he had lost and enriched his walk with Him.

God can bring you through your time of testing and temptation with great victory, too, if you'll use His way out and not yours.

The Great Escape

*"Let me now give you advice, that you may save
your own life and the life of your son Solomon."*

(1 KINGS 1:12)

Many Christians become flaky when they get into trouble. They don't look to the Lord for a way of escape. Instead, they (or someone they know) cook up a way to bring their adversity to a halt, and it only makes matters worse. Some people will try everything under the sun instead of waiting upon God and asking Him for the solution.

God will cause the sun to stand still and part bodies of water to bring you through your seemingly hopeless circumstances or situations victoriously. The only requirement He has is that you look to Him for His way out of your situation. He desires to be your escape route! There are three implications to me for the word "escape": 1) to be saved by the skin of your teeth; 2) to be smooth like cement; and 3) to give counsel that leads to deliverance.

God talks about escape, and man thinks, "By the skin of my teeth." But God will bring you out with great victory. If you pour cement, you'll find that it moves very rapidly and falls into place quickly, and becomes very solid. When God makes a way of escape for you, He will move rapidly, and it will result in a very solid move.

God can give you a Word that will bring your deliverance. First Kings 1:12 says, *"Let me now give you advice, that you may save your own life and the life of your son Solomon."* In this passage of Scripture, the prophet Nathan was warning Bathsheba that the kingship of her son, Solomon, was about to be stolen because Adonijah had appointed himself king over Israel. It was just a matter of time, Nathan warned, before Adonijah ordered their executions.

Nathan and Bathsheba conceived a plan to go to King David and slyly alert him of Adonijah's plot to become king. David immediately responded and assured her: *"I swore to you by the LORD God of Israel, saying, 'Assuredly Solomon your son shall*

be king after me, and he shall sit on my throne in my place,' so I certainly will do this day" (1 Kings 1:30). David then ordered that Solomon ride on his mule to Gihon, where Zadok the priest was to anoint him king. Then Solomon returned and sat on David's throne. By receiving God's way of escape through the wise counsel of Nathan, the queen defeated the plans of Adonijah, thus saving her life and her son Solomon's life.

Before salvation, the devil had appointed himself king over you and had ordered your execution. But God, who is *"not willing that any should perish"* (2 Peter 3:9), provided Jesus as your way of escape from the clutches of hell. Jesus is your way of escape today, regardless of your situation.

The next time you feel overwhelmed by your circumstances, or you are tempted to fix it yourself, look heavenward and say out loud:

> Dear heavenly Father, I thank you for
> your faithfulness to me and that you are
> fully aware of what I am going through.
> I believe you have already provided a
> means for me to successfully endure this
> and to come out of these circumstances
> triumphantly. In Jesus's name, amen.

Surrender

Grief Relief

"I will turn their mourning to joy, will comfort them,
and make them rejoice rather than sorrow."
(JEREMIAH 31:13)

Everyone has situations occur that cause grief to enter. Grief is a natural, normal response when a loved one dies, a marriage or relationship ends, a dream is shattered, or when you feel shame for a mistake. Plus, when we look at recent current events—the ravages of the pandemic, wars and rumors of war, civil unrest and rebellion, escalating tensions with China, the conflict in the Middle East—we feel like the whole nation, if not the world, is grieving! Yet, if you don't deal with your grief, sooner or later, it will steal your happiness, health, success, ministry, and maybe even your life.

How we react to grief determines if it is a good or bad thing in our lives. We can ask God to break our links to past grief, loss, and sin to become fully the person His Word

says we really are. If you become proactive and allow your grief to lead you to God and repentance, He promised, *"To console those who mourn . . . to give them beauty for ashes, the oil of joy for mourning, the garment of praise for the spirit of heaviness"* (Isaiah 61:3). To help you become proactive, I want to give you seven steps to release your grief.

1. **Pray to God:** This isn't a cliché; it's taking the problem to God, as Hannah did (see 1 Samuel 1:15). After prayer, this barren woman received her answer—a baby boy named Samuel, who became a judge and prophet in Israel.

2. **Receive a revelation:** In the throes of grief over the death of his son, Absalom, David was reminded by the Lord through Joab to stop grieving and remember those who had saved his life (see 2 Samuel 19:1–8).

3. **Allow yourself to be comforted:** When the Amalekites invaded Ziklag and took David and his men's families captive, his men spoke of stoning him. But David *"strengthened himself in the LORD his God"* (see 1 Samuel 30:1–6).

4. **Enter into fellowship with God; get resurrection life:** Mary and Martha took their grief to Jesus and received a resurrection miracle (see John 11:19–40).

5. **Repent of sin:** When sorrow or grief is caused by wrongdoing, ask God to forgive you and clean you up (see 2 Corinthians 7:10).

6. **Make your heart merry:** When filled with sorrow, worship will take you into the presence of God, where there is *"fullness of joy"* (see Psalm 16:11).

7. **Know that tribulations work for you:** Paul said to "glory" in your tribulations; God will cause glory and good to come from your sorrow if you hold fast to Him (see Romans 5:3; 2 Corinthians 4:17; Philippians 1:12–13).

A man who attended our church was deserted by his wife for another man. He was devastated by the divorce. While grieving, he asked God to give him a new beginning. The man had never before considered ministry, but God began to open fantastic opportunities for him to minister overseas. He now has an outstanding ministry and a joyful life. What the devil had meant to harm him, God turned to good. In the midst of his sorrow and grief, he sought God for a new beginning. God's answer was beyond anything he could have hoped for. God will do the same for you—if you allow Him to.

Dear friend, use these seven steps to rebound from your grief, for in God, you will find relief. God has promised in Jeremiah 31:13 to *"Turn their mourning to joy, [to] comfort them, and make them rejoice rather than sorrow."*

The Surrendered Life

But God demonstrates His own love toward us, in
that while we were still sinners, Christ died for us.

(ROMANS 5:8)

God offers us total victory in life. Though it's a simple step of faith to reach out and receive from Him, it requires such a total surrender of ourselves that many fail to respond. For example, the rich young ruler came to Jesus and asked what to do to gain eternal life (see Matthew 19:16–22). Jesus demanded of the young man more than he could part with. Jesus didn't care about the man's wealth—He cared about the man. Jesus asked him to give up himself so that Jesus could give him life. The same is still true today. Many of us are willing to give our time, labor, and money to the work of the Lord. But when Jesus asks for ourselves, it's a different story. Yet total surrender to Jesus is where the victorious life comes from.

Only Jesus has the right to ask that we totally surrender to Him because He already surrendered Himself for us. Romans 5:8 tells us that God gave everything for us at the cross: *"But God demonstrates His own love toward us, in that while we were still sinners, Christ died for us."* God says, "I gave everything for you; I totally surrendered. Now you are to be like me. Give me your life."

God isn't asking you to die on a cross to be like Jesus. Jesus already did that! Jesus taught us how to be like Him through total surrender and submission to the Father. He humbled Himself and became like man so that we could become like Him and be exalted. The whole process is summed up in Philippians 2:5–11, which outlines Jesus's seven steps to total surrender and victory.

Verses 6–8 focus on His surrender: Jesus (1) *"Who being in the form of God, (2) did not consider it robbery to be equal with God, (3) but made Himself of no reputation, (4) taking the form of a bondservant, and (5) coming in the likeness of men. (6) And being found in appearance as a man, He humbled Himself (7) and became obedient to the point of death, even the death of the cross."*

You might be asking, "What's so victorious about dying on a cross?" Well, verses 9–11 tell us that after Jesus totally surrendered (died), then God exalted Him in another seven-step process up from the grave: "(1) *Therefore God also has highly exalted Him* (2) *and given Him the name which is above every name,* (3) *that at the name of Jesus every knee should bow,* (4) *of those in heaven,* (5) *and of those on earth,* (6) *and of those under the earth,* (7) *and that every tongue should confess that Jesus Christ is Lord, to the glory of God the Father."*

Godly surrender yields lifetime benefits because it delivers you from the herd attitude that tempts you to say, "I can't do that! What will so-and-so say?" The herd attitude makes us embarrassed to show others that we are surrendered to God. It's the world's attitude of "If it feels good, do it." But folks, if you're a part of the herd, you are surrendered to the herd; and if you're part of them, who's going to minister to the herd?

Instead of a herd attitude, develop your "Word" attitude. The "Word" attitude is just what it says. If the Word says, "Do it," do it!" When you surrender to the cross, then you can be a blessing to others and to yourself because you'll reap what you sow. If you sow forgiveness, you'll reap forgiveness. If you sow love, you'll reap love. God forgave you so you can forgive others. He waited for you to surrender to Him, so now you can patiently minister Him to others and enjoy the fruit of your labors as the whole cycle starts over again with someone to whom you ministered.

Empowered to Do the Supernatural

We have shared together the blessings of God, both when I was in prison and when I was out, . . . telling others about Christ."

(PHILIPPIANS 1:7 TLB)

*A*s diverse as our world is, there is one thing everybody, including you, desires—a full, rich, rewarding, productive, powerful life. The desire for God's best is built into the hearts of every human being. We want loving relationships, peace, significance, purpose, good health, and abundant provision. These desires are not shallow—they are based on the very image and plan of God. Our "instinct" is to "think big," as though nothing were impossible. That's perfect because God has promised that everything *is* possible with Him (see Luke 1:37). The power we need comes from God! He is our source.

God's anointing enabled Aaron to act supernaturally. God told Moses to consecrate Aaron as High Priest by anointing him: *"And you shall take the anointing oil, pour it on his head, and anoint him"* (Exodus 29:7). Psalm 133:2 pictures the anointing oil flowing from the head down: *"Precious oil upon the head, running down on the beard. . . [to] the edge of his garments."* Jesus is our High Priest and our head. We are His body. Just as the oil flowed from Aaron's head to his body, the anointing flows from Jesus to believers.

Jesus's disciples were ordinary men—fishermen, tax collectors, and manual laborers. Jesus transformed them into world-changers. He told His team to *"Go into all the world and preach the gospel to every creature"* (Mark 16:15). That was humanly impossible, yet world history and the Bible confirm that they did indeed "turn the world upside down"! Their credentials didn't enable them to be effective. It was the power and anointing that resulted from their vital connection and partnership with Jesus that empowered them to revolutionize the world—forever! And, God gets all the glory because only He can empower ordinary people to do extraordinary things.

Paul spoke to his partners regarding this transference of the blessings upon his ministry: *"We have shared together the blessings of God, both when I was in prison and when I was out, . . . telling others about Christ"* (Philippians 1:7 TLB). Paul's partners shared his blessing because they were "on his team."

Whatever Paul did, his partners had a part in it as well. Whatever fruit resulted from his ministry was their fruit, too! His reward was their reward. The anointing on his life was on their lives because they entered into partnership with Him.

The disciples became involved in a vision that superseded their thinking. They partook of the anointing, and it overcame their limitations. They stepped up to a level they had not dared to imagine. Following his salvation and anointing, Paul, too, partnered with several people: Barnabas, Silas, Timothy, Titus, Priscilla, and Aquila, to name a few—and with their help and support, spread the gospel to the gentile world. He even wrote half of the New Testament! These men found the power in partnering with Jesus and others.

God didn't create you for a life bound by your own abilities and resources. You, too, can rise to a new level of power, significance, and prosperity! You already have the anointing as a Christian. So, get involved with others in doing the Lord's work. We're all in this together!

Wrestling or Nestling?

*"O Jerusalem, Jerusalem, . . . How often I wanted to
gather your children together, as a hen gathers her
brood under her wings, but you were not willing!"*

(LUKE 13:34)

I'm sure you've seen a little kid running themselves ragged, and then they go and curl up in their daddy's lap, lean their heads against his chest, and nestle up as close as possible. We need to be more like that. We wrestle and wrestle and just wear ourselves out fighting the devil, coming against his work, and proclaiming our victory. But are we getting up in the lap of our heavenly Father and nestling—resting in Him? Don't get me wrong! We are called to do battle with the enemy for the souls of men and for our inheritance in Christ, but if *all* we do is wrestle, we're going to get tired, make mistakes, and maybe burn out.

Have you ever said or thought, "Being a Christian is too hard"? Maybe you should take some time out—stop wrestling with the devil and start nestling with God!

The word *nestle* has in it the word "nest." When we get into God's nest and nestle up to Him, He will "hatch" revelation knowledge in us. Nestling or nesting is nothing new to God;

it's the way He operates. Genesis tells us that at creation, the Holy Spirit "brooded" over the waters that covered the earth. He was "nesting" over the earth. The result was life—hatched on the land and in the sea. The Holy Spirit "overshadowed" Mary, and Jesus was born. When Jesus mourned over Jerusalem, He said, *"O Jerusalem, Jerusalem, . . . How often I wanted to gather your children together, as a hen gathers her brood under her wings, but you were not willing!"* (Luke 13:34). He was saying, "Oh, Jerusalem, if you would have come under my wings and nestled with me, you would have had the revelation that I am your Messiah."

I believe that many times the Lord would love to give us a special revelation—the answer we so desperately desire—but we are so busy wrestling that we don't have time to nestle and allow Him to hatch the answer in us. God will give you revelation knowledge as you *nestle* in Him and study his Word.

Remember when you were first saved how you would snuggle as close to God as you could? How you would spend as much time with Him as possible? How you couldn't wait to get into His presence because you felt so safe and loved there? Friend, He hasn't moved out of the nest—we have; and He is waiting for us to return. Isn't it time to take a break from "wrestling" and return to "nestling"? You are never too old to nestle with Father God. He is waiting for you!

Return to Your First Love

"I counsel you to buy from Me gold refined in the
fire, that you may be rich; and white garments,
that you may be clothed, that the shame of your
nakedness may not be revealed; and anoint
your eyes with eye salve, that you may see."
(REVELATION 3:18)

Have you ever felt you don't have the same zeal for the things of the Lord as you did when you were first saved? Are you lax regarding time spent with Him in His Word? Are the things of this world taking precedence over the things of God in your life? If so, return to your first love—Jesus.

When we are first born-again, we fall in love with Jesus; He becomes the all-consuming passion in our lives. But sometimes, we lose that passion, and He becomes our pastime rather than our passion. In other words, we

become lukewarm as described in Revelation 3:17, *"Because you say, 'I am rich, have become wealthy, and have need of nothing'—and do not know that you are wretched, miserable, poor, blind, and naked."* God says the lukewarm Christian is so blinded he thinks he doesn't need anything and that He will vomit him out of His mouth (see Revelation 3:16). Fortunately, God has provided a solution!

The remedy for being poor, blind, and naked can restore us to the place God desires for us:

> *"I counsel you to buy from Me gold refined in the fire, that you may be rich; and white garments, that you may be clothed, that the shame of your nakedness may not be revealed; and anoint your eyes with eye salve, that you may see."* **(REVELATION 3:18)**

God's solution is "gold tried in the fire." True gold is God's Word. Every believer who has received an answer to prayer has experienced "gold tried in the fire." Remember, when you *"press toward the goal for the prize of the upward call of God in Christ"* (Philippians 3:14), you are pressing toward and pursuing a passion for Jesus, not a pastime. The more you press into Jesus, the more you want to study His Word. The cure for the lukewarm Christian is to take hold of the Word of God.

God offers us white garments, robes of righteousness, as the cure for "nakedness" (Revelation 3:18). First John 3:7 says, *"Let no one deceive you. He who practices righteousness is righteous, just as He is righteous."* You can't lead a secret life in which you go to church on Sundays but are sexually immoral the rest of the week. You may think nobody knows it, but God knows it! That's being lukewarm, and the lukewarm person misses a life of abundance, health, and harmony.

Lukewarm Christians really don't see what God is doing spiritually. They come and do their little church thing and read their Bibles some, but they don't see things as God sees them.

God provides eye salve to cure any blindness. The Word is God's cure, His eye salve for spiritual blindness—so we can see ourselves as God sees us.

God loves us enough to correct us, and He knows how to change a lukewarm heart! Jesus said, *"As many as I love, I rebuke and chasten. Therefore be zealous and repent"* (Revelation 3:19). "Zealous" means "to be heated or to boil in the pursuit of good." And, "zealous" and "jealous" have the same meanings in the Bible. Therefore, the church that is zealous for God is a church that is jealous for God's work. That's the kind of church God wants and what He wants for you. If you repent and take hold of His Word and His righteousness, use the garment and eye salve that He provides, you will see the way He sees, and you will return to your first love.

The Gift of Righteousness

*For with the heart one believes unto righteousness, and
with the mouth confession is made unto salvation.*
(ROMANS 10:10)

Discovering God's gift of righteousness can change your life! I was born-again when I was 16. After all these years of serving God, reading through the Bible countless times, memorizing whole books of the Bible, and ministering around the world, I am no more righteous than I was on the day of my salvation. Righteousness isn't earned or even developed—it's a gift that we receive. This gift—righteousness through Jesus Christ—gives us the power to rule and reign over the situations in our lives.

Have you noticed that you must "believe" and "confess" salvation before you receive it? *"For with the heart one believes unto righteousness, and with the mouth confession is made unto salvation"* (Romans 10:10). When you confess Jesus as Savior, something happens inside—you receive His nature, the nature of righteousness.

When people ask, "How are you?" don't make the mistake of confessing your old nature. Rather, believe and confess your new one.

Instead of saying, "I'm weak, stupid, always blowing it, poor, and sick," say, "I am the righteousness of God in Christ Jesus. Because of righteousness, I rule and reign over every circumstance of my life." If questioned about your weaknesses, say, "I have God's righteousness to overcome all things!"

Don't say or believe that sickness, poverty, bondages, or any other negative things rule your life. Instead, declare that you reign over every obstacle because of His righteousness at work in you. Your confession will bring possession!

Have you heard the story of the man who bought a beautiful, powerful, new car? The man loved his car but never had it serviced. After a couple of years, it would hardly make it up a hill. Finally, he took it in to be checked and discovered that he was driving on only half the cylinders!

Some Christians remember the "good old days" when they were first saved. Like the man with the new car, things were great, and God worked powerfully in their lives. Yet today, every problem is like a mountain. They are trying to travel through life on half their cylinders. They have forgotten that through *the gift of righteousness* [they can] *reign in life*" (Romans 5:17 NIV).

Recognize your righteousness, and *"be renewed in the spirit of your mind, and that you put on the new man which was created according to God, in true righteousness and holiness"* (Ephesians 4:23–24). When your righteousness becomes a literal truth to you, feelings of inferiority fade away, fear of failure flees, and faith for victory arises.

The Gift of Encouragement

Therefore comfort each other and edify one another.

(1 THESSALONIANS 5:11)

The gift of encouragement is important because all believers need encouragement: *"Therefore comfort each other and edify one another"* (1 Thessalonians 5:11). Acts 4:36 tells us of Joses, who operated in the gift of encouragement. Joses was a wealthy priest from Cyprus who got saved and gave his wealth to help persecuted believers. He was such an encouragement that the disciples called him "Barnabas," which means "Son of Encouragement." By encouraging others, we not only uplift them, but we establish areas of service that minister to generations of people after us. Barnabas operated in such a ministry.

When the Holy Spirit called Paul and Barnabas to be missionaries, John Mark went along to serve and learn from them (see Acts 12:25; 13:2). Though called to the ministry, he was still young, immature, and unprepared for the hardships that a missionary had to endure. He ended up going home mid-journey. That's why on their second mission trip, Paul didn't want John Mark to come along, so they separated. Barnabas took John Mark with him. This time, John Mark didn't run home. Barnabas encouraged, trained, and discipled him because he saw who John Mark could be: a hardworking, seasoned minister. John Mark became a very successful minister of the gospel—he wrote the book of Mark. Through this episode with John Mark, even Paul learned the profound results that encouragement could bring. John Mark was with Paul during his first Roman imprisonment (Colossians 4:10; Philemon 24). At the end of his life, Paul sent for John Mark because he was so useful (2 Timothy 4:11).

Like Paul, we may forsake other people because they have disappointed us in the past, but we can also learn to minister encouragement. How? By applying three simple keys found in Hebrews 10, you can unfold your gift of encouragement.

1. **Draw near to God.** Hebrews 10:22 tells us to *"draw near with a true heart in full assurance of faith."* To encourage others successfully, you must first draw near to God and fellowship with Him daily. People who are experiencing difficulties need to hear encouragement that comes straight from Jesus's heart— not something we think He might say.

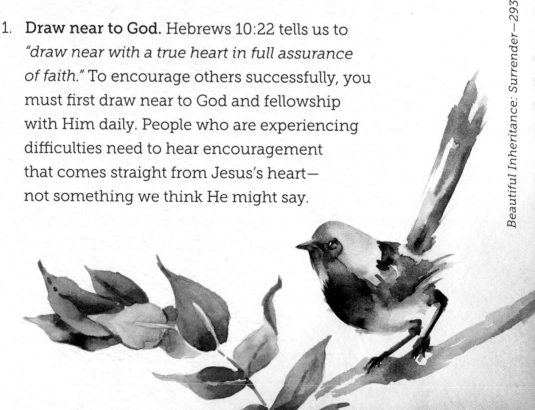

2. **Develop patience.** Fellowship with the Lord gives a spiritual foundation upon which to base a ministry of encouragement. However, it's crucial that we don't allow impatience to erode that foundation: *"Let us hold fast the confession of our hope without wavering, for He who promised is faithful"* (Hebrews 10:23). Unfortunately, most of us begin to lose patience if we don't see results in ten seconds or less. We must wait patiently and steadfastly for answers.

3. **Determine needed actions.** Hebrews 10:24 states, *"And let us consider one another in order to stir up love and good works."* We can speak encouraging words all day, but if they don't instill in others the faith to act, we have wasted our time. To inspire someone to act, remember that *"Faith comes by hearing, and hearing by the Word of God"* (Romans 10:17). The Word of God, the most powerful force in the universe, will instill faith in people's hearts and encourage them to act. Our responsibility is simply to speak forth the Word.

Remember, everyone needs encouragement. Begin today to share your gift of encouragement, and you'll bless the body of Christ for many generations.

Blessings from Being Willing

"Take from among you an offering to the LORD.
*Whoever is of a **willing** heart,"... The children of*
Israel brought a freewill offering to the LORD, all
*the men and women whose hearts were **willing***
to bring material for all kinds of work.
(EXODUS 35:5, 29, EMPHASIS ADDED)

When my husband and I first started pastoring a church of about 40 or 50 people, we really needed a car and began to save for it. We managed to save around $1,000, but before we could spend the money on a car, God impressed Wally to sow that $1,000 into the ministry of T.L. and Daisy Osborn. I grumbled to the Lord about it, but not long after that, John Osteen came to our church. We never mentioned it to him, but during the service, he said, "Wally, I see the letters "C-A-R" over your head; do you need a car?" "Kind-of," was all Wally could reply. That night an offering was taken, and with a little additional money, we were able to buy a car.

However, the harvest from sowing into their evangelistic ministry didn't stop there! Some years later, Daisy spoke at my first women's convention. She raised a tremendous offering for Ethiopia and gave $5,000 to it herself! Then, at another conference in California, she took an offering for a second trip I was taking to Ethiopia and raised $50,000. The harvest from sowing that first $1,000 continued. She came to a meeting I had in St. Louis and took another offering for a mission project and, out of her own pocket, gave $10,000! I asked God, "Is *all* this the result of that first seed we sowed?" "Marilyn," He explained, "I have a supernatural harvest plan. If anyone sows *willingly* into My kingdom, they'll reap a supernatural harvest that will never quit!"

The keyword in all of this, of course, is *willingly*. I could tithe and give offerings, but not do it willingly. I could give alms because I know that I am supposed to yet hate doing it. But if I do those things *willingly*, God will send a continual harvest of good things into my life. One of the best examples of this is when the Israelites were asked to give toward the building of the tabernacle:

*"Take from among you an offering to the LORD. Whoever is of a **willing** heart,"... Then everyone came whose heart was stirred, and everyone whose spirit was **willing**, ... They came, both men and women, as many as had a **willing** heart, ... The children of Israel brought a freewill offering to the LORD, all the men and women whose hearts were **willing** to bring material for all kinds of work.* (EXODUS 35:5, 21–22, 29, EMPHASIS ADDED)

These people were so willing to give that they had to be told to stop giving! (See Exodus 36:6.) And what about the nonstop harvest they received as a result of their giving? Let's look at the record: they traveled in the wilderness for 40 years, and they never had a grocery bill for God fed them! They never had a water bill. God supplied their water! They never needed a pair of shoes. God provided supernaturally for them. They never paid a heating bill. God gave them a pillar of fire for heat at night and a pillar of cloud by day for air conditioning. And they never paid a dime for a defense budget. God was their protection.

Do you think they reaped a nonstop harvest because they gave to build the Lord's house? Yes! But only because they gave *willingly*. And if you and I will allow God to make us willing givers into His kingdom, there is no end to the harvest of blessings that God will pour into our lives.

Giving of Yourself

*Praise ye the LORD for the avenging of Israel, when
the people willingly offered themselves.... My heart is
toward the governors of Israel, that offered themselves
willingly among the people. Bless ye the LORD.*

(JUDGES 5:2, 9 KJV)

Tithing is a touchy subject with some people, especially with non-tithers! The truth is, however, that you can't afford *not* to tithe. That is ten percent of your income that God *requires*, and I don't say that because I was a pastor's wife.

I started tithing when I was 11 years old. My family lived on an apple farm in Pennsylvania, and I sold apples in a little stand out by the road. Although I wasn't a born-again believer at that time, I still tithed on what I made selling apples—and God blessed me for it! I began to get all kinds of baby-sitting jobs, and all through high school, I always had a job and money to spend.

When I was 16, I met the Lord—now I really gave my tithe with a willing heart. I had discovered the law of sowing and reaping, and I put it to work for me as I paid my own way through college, bought my own clothes, and whatever else

I needed. I learned that when you sow into God's kingdom, you reap over and over again. That's why I'm sold on tithing—because it's God's prosperity plan! We should also consider the joy of giving offerings and alms and supporting missionaries who are out there on the front lines.

Additionally, I want you to consider this. Sometimes money is not what God wants us to give; He also wants us to give ourselves, maybe even step out of our comfort zones. Once when I went to South Korea for Dr. Cho's "Church Growth International Conference," I was alone and felt awkward for a time. The Lord told me to look for someone else who might be feeling awkward. I saw someone standing alone and went over to introduce myself. We began to visit, and before long, the person said, "I'm so glad you introduced yourself; I was feeling so uncomfortable here." *I was, too,* I thought. But if you sow friendship, you'll reap friendship. Likewise, if you are willing to give yourself to whatever the Lord asks you to do, you'll reap a nonstop harvest of blessings.

Deborah, a judge of Israel in the days before the Jews had a king, discovered just how much God was willing to do for the people of Israel when they willingly gave themselves to

Him. When the nation of Israel came under the rule of the Canaanites, God performed a mighty deliverance through Deborah, but she couldn't have overcome Sisera and his 900 iron chariots without the Israelites first having offered themselves to the Lord. In their victory song, Deborah and Barak sang: *"Praise ye the* LORD *for the avenging of Israel, when the people willingly offered themselves. . . . My heart is toward the governors of Israel, that offered themselves willingly among the people. Bless ye the* LORD*"* (Judges 5:2, 9 KJV). Whenever we willingly give ourselves to God, He willingly gives Himself back to us so that we have an abundance of peace and prosperity.

Some of you are not willing to let go of the wealth God has enabled you to accumulate, but if you are willing to allow God to change your heart, then that's the most important thing. Allow God to give you a willing heart to sow into His kingdom. In addition, share your abilities and talents with your local church or other ministries: volunteer on the mission committee; help in the nurseries and Sunday school classes; lead a Bible study group. Then sit back and watch how God blesses you!

You Must Remember This

"These stones shall be for a memorial
to the children of Israel forever."

(JOSHUA 4:7)

God likes to remind His people of certain things. Jesus has given Christians two very special things to remember, and if we keep both of these things in mind, we can have victory over past failures, victory over present circumstances, and victory every day throughout our lives.

Remember how the Israelites crossed the Jordan River into the promised land? The waters miraculously parted, and they walked across. Then God told Joshua to set up two memorials of 12 large stones; one was in the midst of the river, and one was on the riverbank (Joshua 4:20). The stones were to be memorials to the Israelites so that:

"When your children ask in time to come, saying, 'What do these stones mean to you?' Then you shall answer them that the waters of the Jordan were cut off before the ark of the covenant of the LORD; . . . these stones shall be for a memorial to the children of Israel forever." **(JOSHUA 4:6–7)**

The heap of stones at the site where they crossed the Jordan was to remind them of all the miracles God wanted to work on their behalf in the present and the future. They were to keep their eyes on God's miracles and His promises—and never look back at the past. They were constant reminders of God's miraculous care and provision. Each time they saw the memorials, their faith would increase, and increased faith meant increased victory.

God's two memorials for Christians are designed the same way. The first memorial is baptism. In John 1:28, we learn that John baptized Jesus in the Jordan River at Bethabara.

Bethabara means "house of the ford or passage." I believe this is where the Israelites crossed the Jordan. Jesus went there to be baptized by John. The one who is *"the way, the truth, and the life"* (John 14:6) went under the waters, which pictures His death for you and me. But that's not all. You were buried with Jesus—that is what your baptism symbolizes: *"buried with Him in baptism"* (Colossians 2:12). That's how God transformed your past—He eliminated it!

The second memorial that Christians celebrate is communion. First Corinthians 11:26 tells us that in communion, we remember not only the Lord's death but also His second coming: *"For as often as you eat this bread and drink this cup, you proclaim the Lord's death till He comes."* In communion, we have a reminder of the daily power needed to live a victorious life (Christ's life within) and the glorious future that awaits us (Christ's second coming).

Like Israel, God has forgiven our past and provided for present and future needs in our lives. Sometimes we forget that God has done everything He can do to ensure we live triumphant Christian lives. That's when we need to take a long look at the two memorials God placed in our lives: baptism and communion. When you recall that your past, present, and future are taken care of by the death, resurrection, and return of Jesus, your faith will increase, and your life will be transformed.

Eternity
with
God

Celebrate Communion

For as often as you eat this bread and drink this cup,
you proclaim the Lord's death till He comes.

(1 CORINTHIANS 11:26)

Did you know that communion releases God's power into your life and declares your relationship with Jesus? It is your truest expression of faith and an intimate form of worship; it's a celebration of new life in Christ and an acceptance of His healing, nourishing power in your life. And it proclaims to the

devil that he is defeated and that he no longer has an open door to bring mental, physical, or spiritual sickness into your body. Communion is much more than simply receiving the elements of juice and bread. When we partake of communion, we proclaim our worthiness—accepting the righteousness of God, which is in Christ Jesus. Unfortunately, many people do not really understand the spiritual and physical impact that communion can have in their lives.

> *Jesus . . . took bread; and when He had given thanks, He broke it and said, "Take, eat; this is My body which is broken for you; do this in remembrance of Me." In the same manner He also took the cup . . . saying, "This cup is the new covenant in My blood. This do, as often as you drink it, in remembrance of Me." For as often as you eat this bread and drink this cup, you proclaim the Lord's death till He comes.* (1 CORINTHIANS 11:23–26)

When Paul wrote to the Corinthians, he was explaining both the process and the result. When he says, *"You proclaim the Lord's death till he comes,"* he places you right in the middle of the action—proclaiming, announcing, declaring, and spiritually shouting to the devil that your sins are forgiven, and you are redeemed! Communion announces to the devil that you're a winner, that he can't defeat you, and that he is a vanquished foe! Through communion, you proclaim to the devil that you have power over him.

This announcement also declares that your body belongs to Jesus. It shouts to the devil and to the world that you've made a choice to accept the life that Jesus offers and the healing that resides within Him. After all, He came to give you abundant life (see John 10:10).

Paul stressed that we be prepared to receive communion: *"But let a man examine himself, and so let him eat of the bread and drink of the cup"* (1 Corinthians 11:28). This doesn't mean that we go over our past sins. When Jesus is your Lord and Savior, He obliterates those sins! Psalm 103:12 says: *"As far as the east is from the west, so far has He removed our transgressions from us."* Rather, Paul talks about the *way* you partake of communion. Are you taking it in faith? Hebrews 11:6 tells us that we can't please God without faith. When you take communion, you are expressing your faith in God, and this brings Him great pleasure. In that environment, you can earnestly seek God's restoration and healing in your life, publicly announce your faith in Jesus, and receive the rewards He has set before you. When you acknowledge that you are a new creation, you demonstrate that you are worthy of stepping into the presence of God.

Next time you're mentally or physically sick, receive communion as a celebration of God's healing power. Tell the devil that he is conquered! Then receive Jesus's mercy and grace and allow His life-changing, life-giving love to *fill* every part of you.

Bring Back the Joy!

Weeping may endure for a night, but
joy comes in the morning.

(PSALM 30:5)

I s there some area of your life where you've lost your joy? Far too many of us find ourselves robbed of one of the most valuable assets available—our joy. In many cases, it's the devil who is to blame. If the devil can take your joy, then he can get to your possessions, your health, your spiritual wellbeing, your strength, and more. I'm flat out mad at him, while my spirit is stirred with compassion for those of you who've been recently attacked by him. It's time to bring the joy back!

The true definition of joy differs from that of "happiness." Happiness can be a fleeting, temporal condition that depends upon the comfort of your flesh. Joy is not based on outward circumstances but upon the condition of your heart and the spiritual stance you take when you have been attacked by the enemy.

I realize that you may be sitting there right now in the middle of a problem. You may even feel as though it will never be over. But, dear friend, Psalm 30:5 reminds us, *"Weeping may endure for a night, but joy comes in the morning."*

If you are a person of faith (even a mustard seed of faith), it doesn't matter how dark conditions may be right now. You can rest assured, your brighter day is on the way! Regardless of how dark or bleak things may seem right now—even if circumstances are devastating—God's joy can be yours!

It's time to knock down the gates of hell that have built up joy-robbing strongholds in your life. It's that plain and simple. You can experience some substantial victories in your circumstances, in Jesus's name. So, here's what I want you to do:

1. Bombard the gates of hell with your prayers! Your joy *is* coming back! Use your faith, your authority, the anointing that's resting on you as a Christian, and the Word of God to activate the weapons of your warfare. That's why 1 John 3:8 says, *"For this purpose the Son of God was manifested, that He might destroy the works of the devil."*

2. Step out in faith and give a gift of faith and joy to someone in need. I have found that the quickest way to get a miracle rejuvenation of joy is by opening your heart and giving the best gift you can—and it doesn't have to be money. Shovel someone's sidewalk, offer to watch their kids, take some cookies to a neighbor, pick up groceries for a lonely senior citizen—whatever you can give, give.

Now believe for breakthrough miracles to be released in your life and circumstances—and watch the joy return!

Joy Makes Life Worth Living

This is the day the LORD has made;
we will rejoice and be glad in it.

(PSALM 118:24)

Our God is a joyful God, and it is with His joy that we become stronger, more powerful Christians. Joy helps you worship God, and it makes you glad, cheerful, and a delight to be around.

You receive the joy of the Lord when you are anointed with the Holy Spirit. This anointing starts at the top of your head and goes all the way to your feet: *"It is like the precious oil upon the head, . . . Running down on the edge of his garments"* (Psalm 133:2). God begins with your head because your thought life gives you direction to set you on the right path.

When you are baptized in the Spirit and receive the anointing, you will act joyful, which is very scriptural. Psalm 66:1 (KJV) says, *"Make a joyful noise unto God."* The Hebrew word for *joyful* is *renânâh*, which means "shout for joy, singing, triumphing." Joyful expressions are loud and noisy. The joy that the Holy Spirit places inside you has to come bubbling out. Romans 14:17

says the kingdom of God *"is righteousness and peace and joy in the Holy Spirit."* If you are moving in the Holy Spirit, you will have the joy that comes with Him.

As a Christian, God calls you to be joyful. Isaiah 51:11 says we will, *"Come to Zion with singing, with everlasting joy on* [our] *heads.* [We] *shall obtain joy and gladness."* The redeemed are supposed to have so much joy it comes out of their mouths. We must be joyful in order to give glory to God and to witness to the lost.

You must commit to daily maintenance of joy. Isaiah 12:3 says, *"Therefore with joy you will draw water from the wells of salvation."* When Jesus lives in your heart, then you already have joy inside. All you have to do is pull some out every day. The fullness of joy is found in God's presence, so start your day by entering into His presence with joy and praise. When you wake up, say, *"This is the day the LORD has made; we will rejoice and be glad in it"* (Psalm 118:24).

If you're not diligent, you can lose your joy. In Psalm 51:12, David said, *"Restore to me the joy of Your salvation"* after he had an affair with Bathsheba and had Uriah killed. He lost his joy because of sin, and the same thing can happen to us. With repentance, God's joy returns. David knew that his salvation would restore his joy. There is no question that David's joy returned—he remained a man after God's own heart, and God sent the Messiah through his lineage.

Don't let problems overcome you; instead, let God's promises take over your problems. God wants you to be joyful in times of trouble, because the strength found in joy will bring you through your problems. Ask the Holy Spirit to anoint you again to resurrect your joyful heart.

According to John 10:10, Jesus came that you may have abundant life. This is the level of blessing that God wants for us. When we decide to be led by a joyful heart, strive to joyfully express our love for God, and commit to maintaining our joy by seeking God daily, God's true power can be released—and we can have the overflowing abundance of joy the Word promises.

Your Finest Hour

"Lift up your eyes and look at the fields,
for they are already white for harvest."
(JOHN 4:35)

very nation has moments when it is receptive to the gospel. Jesus said to His disciples, *"Lift up your eyes and look at the fields, for they are already white for harvest"* (John 4:35). At the end of World War II, General MacArthur cried out to church leaders, "Send 5,000 missionaries to Japan!" Japan was wide open to the gospel, but only 150 missionaries responded. When the explorer Marco Polo met Genghis Kahn—an early ruler of China—and gave him the gospel, Genghis Khan said, "Send 1,000 missionaries to teach my people about Jesus." Only 50 responded. What would China be like today if it had become a Christian nation back then?

God uses ordinary people to do what others only think about doing. They sacrifice themselves—their time, energy, fortunes, and even their reputations—to rescue souls from hell. God wants you to do more than you have ever done before. Today, more than ever, we need a fresh move of the Holy Spirit to envelop our nation.

We have gone through tumultuous times lately. We suffered through 9/11. We have seen our nation torn apart by political and civil strife; unprecedented crime and murders dominate the news. COVID-19 ravaged America (and the world), totally uprooting a way of life that was the envy of the world. I believe America's "pocket of time" has come. It is time to get serious about our relationship with God. I believe it is time for revival!

Now is the time to:

1. **Go to church.** If you don't already attend a church regularly, find a Bible-believing church. Become active and take your place in the body of Christ.

2. **Read the Bible.** Begin a daily Bible reading plan if you don't have one already. God's Word is your greatest shield and mightiest weapon; you must know it and learn to use it. (You can start now! **Find complimentary Bible Reading Plans at marilynandsarah.org**)

3. **Pray.** If you don't have a regular, daily time when you pray and talk to God, rearrange your schedule. Folks, do whatever it takes to deepen your relationship with God! Your country and our leaders need your prayers.

4. **Impart peace.** Many people in our country are wounded and filled with fear for the future. Jesus promised His people peace, *"Peace I leave with you, My peace I give to you; not as the world gives do I give to you. Let not your heart be troubled, neither let it be afraid"* (John 14:27). Establish God's peace in your heart by entrusting your future into His care. Then become an ambassador of God's peace—share it with others.

5. **Get right with God.** Some of you have been "playing around" with spiritual things. You're straddling the fence—one leg in the world and one in church. If you would like to dedicate or rededicate your life completely to God, pray this prayer:

> God, forgive my sins. Forgive me for playing around with worldly things and for treating you lightly. I turn my back on sin, and I dedicate my life to you. Help me to become *all* that you have called me to be. Amen.

This is your "pocket of time." What will you do? Will you become a "reaper," a hero in the revival harvest? This could be your finest hour—*if* you make it so!

The Start of Something Wonderful

"Now when these things begin to happen, look up and lift up your heads, because your redemption draws near."

(LUKE 21:28)

*A*re we living in the "end times"? How close are the "last days"? Are America and the world poised at a defining moment in history? Are the nations of the world forming political alliances in fulfillment of end-time prophecies? I believe these are the end times, but it is not a season to fear but a time to rejoice! Jesus said, *"Now when these things begin to happen, look up and lift up your heads, because your redemption draws near"* (Luke 21:28).

September 11, 2001, changed our world. It polarized nations into a struggle between good and evil. Sooner or later, an association of countries will emerge and evolve into the empire of the Antichrist. That area will be the stage upon which key end-time events take place. The Antichrist will try to rule the entire world, but he will only succeed in bringing the nations of the former Roman Empire under his control. Eventually, he will bring temporary peace to a world weary of war. Then, many will hail him as a man of peace. The whole world will adore him—even Israel will be deceived and believe he is their Messiah (see Daniel 7 and Revelation 13 and 17).

Before the Antichrist takes power, millions of Christians (but not all) will be removed from our planet. The rapture is beautifully pictured in chapter 12 of Revelation. The church is portrayed as a pregnant woman clothed with the brilliance of the sun, whose feet rest upon the moon and whose head is surrounded by 12 stars. Pictured as a red dragon, Satan is waiting to pounce upon her. When she gives birth to the "overcoming church," it is immediately taken up—raptured—to heaven. The woman, the lukewarm church, flees to hide herself.

We need to make certain that we are part of the overcoming church. The lukewarm church will not go to heaven in the pre-tribulation rapture. It must endure three-and-a-half years of the darkest, most difficult period in human history—the tribulation—which begins in earnest when the peace of the

Antichrist is abruptly shattered. He will desecrate the rebuilt temple in Jerusalem with an idol of himself that talks (see Revelation 13:14–15). With this act, the deceived nation of Israel will come to its senses and renounce the Antichrist. Indwelt by Satan, the Antichrist will become furious with Israel. He will assemble a great army to destroy Israel.

The Battle of Armageddon will be the worst battle in human history. Thousands will die. In the final moments of the war, all will seem to be lost, and the Antichrist will appear to have won. Then, Jesus will break through the clouds with an army of saints. Christ himself will defeat Satan, the Antichrist, and their hordes. The crucial question is, "Where will you be on that day?"

Dear friend, the rapture could occur at any moment. Our world is a dangerous place to be lukewarm in your relationship with God. Now is the time to return to Him and commit your life to God. If you would like to be sure of your relationship with God, pray with me:

> Father God, forgive me of my sins and create in me a clean heart. I turn away from sin and turn to you. I accept Jesus as my Lord and Savior. I give myself completely to you. I want to be a part of your army in the end times. Show me how to serve you at this crucial time. Amen.

Welcome to the start of something wonderful—eternity with your Savior!

Heaven

We know that when He is revealed, we shall be like Him.

(1 JOHN 3:2)

*H*eaven is paradise! It isn't a state of mind or a theme park of streets paved with gold, pearly gates, and chubby cherubs riding on the clouds. It's a beautiful place where you are free from every pain, care, and limitation. Jesus has been preparing a place there for those who have a personal relationship with Him, and once you go, you never have to return to the cares of life!

While many people believe in heaven, few believe in hell. Yet, the same Bible that describes heaven also depicts a terrible place. Hell was prepared for Satan and those who follow him. Anyone who hasn't received salvation through Jesus Christ will

one day step into their worst nightmare. They will take permanent residence in the horrifying halls of hell with Satan and the fallen demons for roommates.

Believe it or not, the church is both a model and an extension of heaven. Furthermore, what goes on in the church should model the activities in heaven:

- Jesus is present in heaven and in the church whenever two or three gather together.
- Worship of God takes place in heaven and in the church.
- Order and organization are found in heaven and in the church.
- Relationships will be made in heaven, and the church was made for relationships.
- Angels can be found in heaven and in the church.
- God's Word is the law in heaven and in the church.
- Heaven and the church are meeting places for God's people.

Your flesh and blood can't make it into heaven. If you are born-again when you die, your reborn spirit will go to heaven, and you will be like Jesus: *"We know that when He is revealed, we shall be like Him"* (1 John 3:2). When Christ returns to Earth, your body will be raised from the dead and changed to be like

His (see 1 Corinthians 15:50–54). You will love that body! Your glorified body will be infinitely better—no more sickness, pain, wrinkles, fat, or gray hair.

There are things that happen on a daily basis in our own lives or on the news that remind us that life is fragile and temporary. Fear of the unknown plagues us. But how long you live isn't as important as where you go when you die. Will you go up to an actual heaven or down to a horrific hell?

No one goes to heaven by accident or default. Only people who have chosen Jesus as their Savior and Lord will have a home in heaven. So, if you were to die this moment, which direction would you go—up or down? I pray I can meet you up there.

Eternity:
Your Inheritance Is Waiting

The heavens were opened and I saw visions of God.

(EZEKIEL 1:1)

Ah! Heaven! You've finally arrived! You now see God face-to-face! What does it look like? What do you see? What are people doing? Obviously, I can't tell you from experience. All I can do is point you to Scripture so you can get a glimmer of its unparalled splendor—of its sights and sounds, and most importantly, of the glory of God.

Jesus told us in the story of Lazarus and the rich man that angels will usher us into the presence of the Lord upon our deaths (see Luke 16:22). I'm pretty sure that Jesus will be first in the reception line of your friends and family who have gone on before you and who are waiting to greet you. After the excitement of being surrounded by the glory of God, and getting up from falling down prostrate before Him, you will begin to look around. I imagine you will see some of the same creatures that Isaiah and Ezekiel saw in their visions of heaven. Isaiah described the throne room in Isaiah 6:1–2:

In the year that King Uzziah died, I saw the Lord
sitting on a throne, high and lifted up, and the
train of His robe filled the temple. Above it stood
seraphim; each one had six wings: with two he
covered his face, with two he covered his feet, and
with two he flew. And one cried to another and said:

"Holy, holy, holy is the LORD of hosts;
The whole earth is full of His glory!"

Above the throne were seraphim—creatures with six wings and that seemed somewhat similar in appearance to humans— they had faces, voices, feet, and hands. Ezekiel also described his vision of four living creatures having the likeness of men. He provided a very lengthy description of them in Ezekiel 1:4–28. These creatures moved through the coordinated efforts of a "wheel within a wheel." In this vision, he also described a throne and the glory of God:

And above the firmament over their heads was the likeness of a throne, in appearance like a sapphire stone; on the likeness of the throne was a likeness with the appearance of a man high above it. Also from the appearance of His waist and upward I saw, as it were, the color of amber with the appearance of fire all around within it; and from the appearance of His waist and downward I saw, as it were, the appearance of fire with brightness all around. Like the appearance of a rainbow in a cloud on a rainy day, so was the appearance of the brightness all around it. This was the appearance of the likeness of the glory of the LORD. **(EZEKIEL 1:26–28)**

In addition to "strange" creatures, Revelation gives us clues as to some of the other things that will be there. The light of heaven emanates from the Lord God Himself (Revelation 22:5). Revelation 21:21 tells us that the gates of the New Jerusalem

will have gates made of single pearls and streets paved with gold. In the middle of one of heaven's streets, we will find the tree of life (Revelation 22:2). Now, there is so much speculation as to where the ark of the covenant is. What happened to it? Well, we know we will see it again because when the temple of God is opened in heaven, we will also see the ark of His covenant in the temple (see Revelation 11:19).

Furthermore, Jesus told us in John 14:2–3 that He is preparing mansions for us. No matter how splendid these buildings may be, the joy of eternally dwelling with Jesus in our Father's house will be the most spectacular thing of all. In communion with the four living creatures and the 24 elders, our unbroken fellowship with Him and other believers will culminate in worship—people from *"every tribe and tongue and people and nation"*—praising our Redeemer (see Revelation 5:8–11).

We also know that there will be no more sickness, disease, hunger, or thirst, no more crying, and no more death. Rather, *"The ransomed of the LORD shall return, and come to Zion with singing, with everlasting joy on their heads. They shall obtain joy and gladness, and sorrow and sighing shall flee away"* (Isaiah 35:10).

What will we do in heaven? Unlike the fairy-tale version of heaven, we will not be sitting on clouds, playing harps. We have assignments to fulfill. There is coming a time when the kindoms of this world shall become the kingdoms of our Lord (Revelation 11:15). Who will rule over these kingdoms? Daniel's prophecy makes it very clear that God's people will rule:

*"But the saints of the Most High shall receive
the kingdom, and possess the kingdom forever,
even forever and ever."... "Then the kingdom and
dominion, and the greatness of the kingdoms
under the whole heaven, shall be given to the
people, the saints of the Most High. His kingdom
is an everlasting kingdom, and all dominions
shall serve and obey Him."* (DANIEL 7:18, 27)

Jesus indicated that authority over cities will be given as a reward to those who have been faithful with what the Lord has given them to do in this world. This is brought out in His parable of the minas, in that those who had performed well were rewarded: *"Well done, good servant; because you were faithful in a very little, have authority over ten cities"* (Luke 19:17).

In addition, Hebrews 2:5–8 makes it clear that men will take part in governing the world to come:

*For He has not put the world to come, of
which we speak, in subjection to angels.
But one testified in a certain place, saying:*

"What is man that You are mindful of him,
Or the son of man that You take care of him?
You have made him a little lower than the angels;
You have crowned him with glory and honor,
And set him over the works of Your hands.
You have put all things in subjection under his feet."

As Christians, we are to be part of God's management of the new heaven and the new earth. The initial phase of this includes participating in God's judgment on the fallen angels. The book of Jude tells us that God has already passed judgment on some of them: *"And the angels who did not keep their proper domain, but left their own abode, He has reserved in everlasting chains under darkness for the judgment of the great day"* (Jude 1:6).

According to Paul's letter to the Corinthians, Christians will join in approving this final sentence of judgment upon the fallen angels: *"Do you not know that the saints will judge the world? And if the world will be judged by you, are you unworthy to judge the smallest matters? Do you not know that we shall judge angels?"* (1 Corinthians 6:2–3).

There certainly is much more that awaits us as we rejoice with our loved ones and other believers in songs of praise to our wonderful God while we judge, rule, and reign with Christ! Oh, what a beautiful inheritance!

RECEIVE JESUS AS LORD
AND SAVIOR OF YOUR LIFE

You can have Jesus's joy, peace, protection, and provision in your life starting today. You can also know for sure that you will have life after death in heaven.

God sent Jesus Christ to be the Savior of the world. First Timothy 2:5–6 says, *"For there is one God and one Mediator between God and men, the Man Christ Jesus, who gave Himself a ransom for all."*

The Bible tells us how we can receive Jesus as Savior:

> *If you confess with your mouth the Lord Jesus and believe in your heart that God has raised Him from the dead, you will be saved. For with the heart one believes unto righteousness, and with the mouth confession is made unto salvation.* (ROMANS 10:9–10)

Would you like to begin a personal relationship with God and Jesus right now? You can! Simply pray this prayer in sincerity:

> Heavenly Father, I acknowledge that I need your help. I am not able to change my life or circumstances through my own efforts. I know that I have made some wrong decisions in my

life, and at this moment I turn away from those ways of thinking and acting. I believe you have provided a way for me through Jesus to receive your blessings and help in my life. Right now, I believe and confess Jesus as my Lord and Savior. I ask Jesus to come into my heart and give me a new life by your Spirit. I thank you for saving me, and I ask for your grace and mercy in my life. I pray this in Jesus's name. Amen.

If you just prayed to make Jesus your Lord, we want to know! Please call us today—toll free—at **888-637-4545**.

We will pray for you and send you a special gift to help you in your new life with Christ.

END NOTES

Hebrew (H) and Greek (G) word definitions from Strong, James. *Strong's Exhaustive Concordance Complete and Unabridged.* Grand Rapids: Baker Book House, 1980.

Day 3. Zealousness

"Zeal"—James Strong, "H7068."

"Rochunga"—Rochunga Pudaite. *Beyond the Next Mountain.* (Colorado Springs: Bibles for the World.)

Day 9. Profiting from Jesus's Ascension

"Advantage" under "Expedient" W.E. Vine, *An Expository Dictionary of New Testament Words.* (Old Tappan: Fleming H. Revell Company), 1966.

Day 11. Renewal

"Renew"—James Strong, "H2498."

Day 14. Be Holy

"Create"—James Strong, "H1254."

Day 28. Forgive and Forget

"Manasseh"—James Strong, "H4519."

"Ephraim"—James Strong, "H669."

Day 29. Standing in the Gap

"Impute"—Psalm 23, footnote "b." Bible Gateway. www.biblegateway.com/passage/?search=psalm+32&version=NKJV

Day 30. How to Make the Most of Your Offenses

"Offense"—James Strong, "G4625," and W.E. Vine, "Offense."

Day 34. Walking in Integrity

"Integrity"—James Strong, "H8537."

Day 42. Hide and Seek

"Effective"—James Strong, "G1754."

Day 47. Hard-to-Love People

"Jezreel"—James Strong, "H3157."

"*Lo-Ruhamah*"—James Strong, "H3819."

"*Lo-Ammi*"—James Strong, "H3818."

Day 48. The Grace Escape

"*Ishi*"—James Strong, "H376."

"*Baali*"—James Strong, "H1180."

Day 77. Pressure? Press into God

"Israel"—James Strong, "H3478."

Day 80. Turning Opposition into Opportunity

"*Esek*"—James Strong, "H6230."

"*Sitna*"—James Strong, "H7856."

Day 89. Return to Your First Love

"Zealous"—Joseph H. Thayer. *Thayer's Greek-English Lexicon of the New Testament*. (Grand Rapids, MI: Baker Book House, 1997), 271.

"Zealous and jealous"—W.E. Vine. *An Expository Dictionary of New Testament Words*. (Old Tappan, NJ: Fleming H. Revell Company, 1966), 249.

Day 94. You Must Remember This

"Bethabara"—Blue Letter Bible. www.blueletterbible.org/lexicon/g962/kjv/tr/0-1/

Day 97. Joy Makes Life Worth Living

"Joyful"—James Strong, "H7445."

ABOUT MARILYN HICKEY

Encouraging, optimistic, always upbeat and energetic, even in her later years, Marilyn Hickey actively ministers internationally. As founder and president of *Marilyn Hickey Ministries*, a non-profit ministry and humanitarian organization based in Denver, Colorado, Marilyn has impacted many countries worldwide—from disaster relief efforts in Haiti, Indonesia, and Pakistan to providing food for the hungry in Mexico, Costa Rica, Russia, and the Philippines.

Her legacy includes significant visits to Islamic countries. In 2016, over one million people attended her healing meeting in Karachi, Pakistan.

Marilyn has held audiences with government leaders and heads of state all over the world. She was the first woman to join the board of directors for Dr. David Yonggi Cho (founder of the world's largest congregation, Yoido Full Gospel Church in South Korea). She has traveled to over 140 countries and plans to minister to more in the years to come.

Along with her daughter, Pastor Sarah Bowling, she co-hosts the daily television program, *Today with Marilyn & Sarah,* which is broadcast globally. *Today with Marilyn & Sarah* is shown in nearly 200 countries with a potential viewing audience of over 2 billion households worldwide. Marilyn has also authored over 100 publications.

She and her late husband, Wallace, were married over 50 years and have two children and four grandchildren. Marilyn holds a Bachelor of Arts in Collective Foreign Languages from the University of Northern Colorado and an Honorary Doctor of Divinity from Oral Roberts University.

In 2015, Marilyn was honored at Oral Roberts University with the prestigious Lifetime Global Achievement Award. This award recognizes individuals, or organizations, that have made a significant impact in the history of ORU and around the world. In 2019, Marilyn also received an International Lifetime Peace Award from the Grand Imam and President of Pakistan.

In 2021, Marilyn was honored with two awards from the Assemblies of God Theological Seminary: The Pillar of Faith Award in acknowledgment of her worldwide impact on the church through biblical teaching and sustainable healing ministry; and the Smith Wigglesworth Award, given on behalf of the entire Assemblies of God fellowship in acknowledgment of her decades of service worldwide.

Marilyn's greatest passion and desire is to continue being a bridge-builder in countries around the world, and she shows no signs of stopping.

NOTES